NINA RAINE

Nina Raine's other plays include *Consent* (National Theatre, London, 2017/Harold Pinter Theatre, West End, 2018), *Tiger Country* (Hampstead Theatre, London, 2011 and 2014), *Tribes* (Royal Court, London, 2010/Barrow Street Theatre, New York, 2012) and an adaptation of *The Drunks* by the Durnenkov Brothers (Royal Shakespeare Company, 2009). She was awarded the 2006 Evening Standard and Critics' Circle Awards for Most Promising Playwright for her debut play *Rabbit*. *Tribes* won the Drama Desk Award for Outstanding Play, the New York Drama Critics' Circle Award for Best Foreign Play and the Off-Broadway Alliance Award for Best New Play. It has also been produced in LA, Chicago, throughout Europe and the rest of the world, having been translated into over ten different languages, including Croatian, Estonian, Italian, German, Hebrew, Hungarian, Japanese, Korean, Portuguese, Spanish and Swedish.

Nina Raine

STORIES

NICK HERN BOOKS
London
www.nickhernbooks.co.uk

A Nick Hern Book

Stories first published in Great Britain as a paperback original in 2018 by
Nick Hern Books Limited, The Glasshouse, 49a Goldhawk Road, London
W12 8QP

Stories copyright © 2018 Nina Raine

Nina Raine has asserted her right to be identified as the author of this work

Cover image by Louis Davies

Designed and typeset by Nick Hern Books, London
Printed in Great Britain by Mimeo Ltd, Huntingdon, Cambridgeshire PE29 6XX

A CIP catalogue record for this book is available from the British Library

ISBN 978 1 84842 795 2

Woodland
CARBON
www.woodlandcarbon.co.uk
NICK HERN BOOKS
Printed on Carbon Captured paper

Stories was first performed in the Dorfman auditorium of the National Theatre, London, on 18 October 2018 (previews from 10 October). The cast was as follows:

ANNA	Claudie Blakley
FELIX/TOM/LACHLAN/ DANNY/CORIN/RUPERT	Sam Troughton
JOE/PETE/JAMES	Brian Vernel
PAUL/DAD	Stephen Boxer
BETH/JULIE	Thusitha Jayasundera
MOTHER/NATASHA/JENNY	Margot Leicester
GIRL	Sylvie Erskine
	Beau Gadsdon
	Katie Simons

Director	Nina Raine
Designer	Jeremy Herbert
Lighting Designer	Bruno Poet
Music and Sound	Alex Baranowski
Movement Director	Jane Gibson
Voice and Dialect Coach	Charmian Hoare
Staff Director	Piers Black

To Misha, Jack and Mo

Characters

ANNA, *late thirties*
FELIX, *late thirties. Art dealer*
JOSEPH, *late twenties. Anna's brother*
DAD, *Anna's dad*
MOTHER, *Anna's mother*
TOM, *middling twenties. Anna's ex-boyfriend*
GIRL, *between six and ten years old*
LACHLAN, *Irish. An actor. Late thirties*
DANNY, *London. A DJ and musician. Late thirties*
CORIN, *a film director. Fifties*
JULIE, *an acquaintance of Anna's. Australian. Fifties*
BETH, *Anna's close friend. Early forties*
PAUL, *a house-husband. Thirties*
RUPERT, *a graphic novelist*
JENNY, *a counsellor*
PETE, *Rupert's boyfriend*
JAMES, *thirties. Nondescript accent*
NATASHA, *Russian. Eighties*

Plus, voice of ZACH, *Anna's brother*

Many of the characters are doubled – and this is partly the point.

This text went to press before the end of rehearsals and so may differ slightly from the play as performed.

Scene One

40

A slightly bare kitchen with lots of pieces of modern art, but rather than being hung on the walls, it is mainly stacked in piles against the skirting. A few sculptures placed here and there.

ANNA wanders around looking at them, unsure whether to sit down or not, while FELIX watches her. ANNA looks up, taking in the height of the room.

ANNA. Yes. It is quite batch, isn't it?

FELIX. Mm. It's not really my style, but it belonged to some banker who did it up and... he wanted a bachelor pad... so...

ANNA. Hence the polished concrete.

FELIX. And LED lights, and...

ANNA. Fridges...

FELIX.... Yes... But then almost immediately he met a woman, had a baby and... not a bachelor any more.
So he put it on the market.

ANNA looks a bit at the art.

ANNA (*kindly*). The art warms it up a *lot*.

FELIX. Oh good.

ANNA. These...

She indicates some copper containers.

Are they art?

FELIX. Not really, I got them at auction, you just end up buying stuff. They're for petrol I think, to tell you you really are buying a gallon and so on.

Beat.

At least someone like Paul Mellon had a cultural intelligence. Some of these Russian oligarchs it's really, it's very depressing, it's, let's just buy another fifty Damien Hirsts kind of thing. They're just plundering. Oil in Russia, a Damien Hirst, it doesn't matter to them.

ANNA is producing a small Carluccio's bag. She takes some gingerbread men out.

ANNA. Well, I bought these from Carluccio's to give a festive feel.

They laugh.

FELIX. Oh, gingerbread men, lovely... Do you want a cup of tea?

ANNA. Oh yes.

Are you having one?

FELIX busies himself with the kettle.

FELIX. No.

ANNA. I don't really *need* one...

FELIX. No, no...

FELIX gets a cup, teabag, etc.

It was good, actually, going to get tested, apparently my hep-C vaccination's about to expire. Anyway I'm fine for anything up to the last six weeks.

Beat.

ANNA (*curiously*)....Have you *had* action in the last six weeks?

FELIX. I have, but very very safe.

ANNA. Wow, action in the last six weeks, well done, you!

FELIX. Well...

ANNA. I haven't had action in the past *year.*

ANNA gets a newspaper out of her bag.

I bought something to read…

Pause.

…Um, Felix – where do you want me to go?

FELIX *galvanises himself.*

FELIX. Yes. What I thought was, I'll go in the bathroom, with some porn. And you can… the bedroom's just here.

He indicates a door, off.

ANNA. Oh great. So I'll just lie down and read the paper sort of thing?

FELIX. Grand. And then I'll bring it in and… you do your stuff. I've got to head out actually. So I'll just leave you there.

Take all the time you want.

ANNA. That's brilliant.

…Actually, could I have a towel?

FELIX. Yes, yes of course…

Let me go and…

He goes off, speaks from off.

Sorry, the room's a bit of a mess…

…My friend was staying… I *have* changed the sheets…

ANNA (*half to herself, she is busy looking through her bag again*).…Oh, thank you…

FELIX (*from off*). Actually, I got some flowers. Daffodils.

ANNA. Oh, how lovely.

FELIX *comes back in. She turns to him questioningly with some syringes in plastic packaging.*

I don't know what size…?

Syringe?

How much do you normally…?

FELIX. Well it depends, really, on how turned on I am.

ANNA picks up one of the metal containers.

ANNA. Not a gallon then.

FELIX (*remembering*).... Your tea!

He makes to resume tea-making, ANNA *looks at her watch.*

ANNA. Actually, Felix – I'm a bit worried, actually, about *time* – do you think we ought to just – ? I can skip the tea.

FELIX abandons tea-making.

FELIX. Yes, yes of course. Of course! I'll go in there.

ANNA. I don't mean to be bossy...

FELIX. No no. I'll get on with it.

As he goes out.

Help yourself to anything you want.

ANNA. Thank you.

We hear the fan turn on as he goes into the bathroom and switches the light on, closes the door.

ANNA is left on her own. She looks around at the art a bit more. Looks off towards the bathroom. Surreptitiously listens to see if she can hear any noises. She can't. Then she hesitantly goes off into the spare bedroom with her bag and newspaper. The room is left empty.

Scene Two

39

ANNA *sits with her brother,* JOSEPH. *They are scrolling through a website on a laptop which they pass between one another. When* ANNA *taps away,* JOSEPH *cranes over her shoulder.*

Their DAD *sits nearby, simultaneously engrossed in his own laptop and an open book beside him. Occasionally he throws comments into the mix but largely stays focused on his work.*

JOSEPH. Fucking hell, that's a bit expensive.

ANNA. Well there's no point doing the cheap one because then you don't get to see their photos.

JOSEPH. Right. So you do a search...

ANNA. Yeah... 'UK-compliant' because it's based in America... (*Filling in details.*) *Any* height, you think, right?

JOSEPH. Well. Beggars can't be choosers.

ANNA. No, I think it's *when* you're a beggar that you should get *really* choosy.

DAD (*half to himself*). It's when you're selling the *Big Issue* you should turn vegan.

ANNA. Race... what should I put?

JOSEPH. 'Any'? 'All'?

ANNA. Well what I'd *like*, in an ideal world, to *maximise* the genetic pool, is go for a Nigerian or something but apparently you're not allowed.

JOSEPH. Seriously? Not allowed to go black?

ANNA. No. If you're white Caucasian you can't go for black, Asian, Chinese...

DAD. This is fucking racist.

ANNA. They think the kid would be fucked up because it would be looking at you thinking, 'Why am I black when Mummy is white?'

DAD. Most people on the bus are thinking that.

JOSEPH. That's *life*, isn't it? 'Why am I thin when Mummy is
fat, why am I thick when Daddy is clever...' It's crazy...
I mean, I don't look anything like Mum or Dad.

ANNA. Yes you do.

You look like Dad.

DAD. / He looks nothing like me.

JOSEPH. /... So unfair! Fuck you.

ANNA. You've got his jaw.

JOSEPH. / Fuck off!

DAD. / Fuck you!

JOSEPH *feels his jaw.*

ANNA. Anyway. I'm going to do a search on *all* races.

She taps at the laptop.

The more the merrier.

She taps away busily.

I mean how can they check that I'm white? If I just buy the
sperm, who's going to be checking?

JOSEPH. That's the first white thing you've done. You've
bought the sperm.

Some results come up with a ping.

ANNA. ...Christ...

JOSEPH. What?

Beat.

ANNA. Only thirty matches.

That are UK-compliant *and* open-identity.

JOSEPH. Open-identity?

ANNA. Willing to be contacted by the child.

JOSEPH *looks*.

(*Winded*.) Fucking hell. Only *thirty*. Jeez.

JOSEPH. Maybe that's because not many want to be contacted…

DAD *looks up from his laptop*.

DAD. Have you taken Daisy out yet?

ANNA. No.

DAD. Well someone needs to take her out for a pee. Are you staying for supper?

JOSEPH. No. We've got to get back to London.

ANNA (*still engrossed in the laptop*). Some of these have good intelligence scores…

DAD. Piss. Who believes '*intelligence* scores'? Philip Tate got a first-class degree – thick as shit! – and a cunt.

ANNA. Well, that's what I've got to go on.

DAD (*rousing himself*). Look. Isn't the whole point to do it with someone interesting? *Interesting* genes? At least Tom was bright.

ANNA. But he left me.

DAD. I know, so fuck him. (*Gestures at her laptop*.) The trouble with this is, you don't know what you're *getting*. What kind of genes. How are you going to know what these people are like from a *website*? You can't meet them, can you?

ANNA. No.

ANNA *is already deep in the profiles.* JOSEPH *looks over her shoulder. The list that comes up does not show any photos – you have to click on a folder to open the photos.*

DAD. You need to *see* what people look like –

ANNA. There are photos.

DAD. – looks can give you a very approximate, not foolproof, but *good* indicator of what you're getting –

JOSEPH. Dad, there are photos –

DAD (*obliviously*). There's a *reason* that murderers are cross-eyed and have low brows, it's nature's way of warning you, and then of course you get Picasso, little and delicious with piercing sexy eyes – but with a sperm bank, it's a spunk in the dark.

ANNA *and* JOSEPH (*in unison*). There are *photos*!!

ANNA. – I mean, some of these are *fantastic* racial mixes… This one's Chinese, Cherokee, Afro-Caribbean. Sounds *gorgeous*. Maybe the baby'll just be a bit tanned.

She clicks on the photo folder. Beat.

JOSEPH. / Definitely black.

ANNA. / That is a very black man.

   ANNA *gets up in frustration.*

   The crazy thing is, in *life*, who's going to stop me going to a barber shop in New Cross and having a one-night stand with a Nigerian?

JOSEPH. The dudes in the barber shops are picky…

ANNA.…And yet, *this* way, you've got to choose someone with the same fucking *eye* colour *and* do therapy and counselling to show you're not fucking mad…!

   JOSEPH *has gone back to the list.*

JOSEPH. Well, you *are* fucking mad…
   What about six-foot-four, / Welsh –

DAD. / Too tall. Won't be clever. Tall people aren't clever.

JOSEPH. – Welsh, German, Israeli, twenty-two years old.

ANNA. Mm, sounds good.

   JOSEPH *clicks on the photo folder. They crane. Pause. He clicks again, through a few photos.*

   (*Grudgingly.*) Well – he's *white*…

   …look at his *T*-shirts…

JOSEPH.…He must *really* like Nirvana…

ANNA. Why is he by a *dumpster*?

JOSEPH. You've got to ask questions when someone's best photo is them by a skip.

ANNA. I suppose he *is* only twenty-two.

He carries on clicking.

JOSEPH. Look. You can look at their letter to the child.

ANNA *takes over, clicks.*

ANNA. 'A letter from Donor 21420.

When you read this I hope it will help you know a bit more about who I am and answer some questions you may have.

JOSEPH *nods, un-judgementally.*

First of all you might want to know why I did this. I believe the gift of life is the best gift one person can give to another. My mother is the most important person in my life to me and if I can help someone become a mother I feel I'm giving something back to her.'

ANNA *has become tearful.*

Oh my God.

JOSEPH. Yeah…

ANNA *struggles with herself, then –*

ANNA. Oh my God… It's so amazing that this… twenty-*two*-year-old can…

DAD. Write so badly?

ANNA. No!! Do this amazing thing, take this leap into the dark… they have no idea where their sperm's going to end up…

DAD. Typical twenty-two-year-old. Irresponsible.

ANNA. And *Tom*…

JOSEPH.…Fucking *twat,* goes *out* with you for three *years,* and hasn't got the fucking *balls*… literally…

DAD. Fair enough. I don't blame him. I didn't want a child when I was Tom's age. I didn't want a child when we had *you*, Anna.

ANNA *blinks the tears back, carries on reading…*

ANNA. 'I am proud to say I was captain of the baseball team for two years in high school, physical exercise has always been important to me and I go kayaking every other day.'

Her tone has shifted from tearful to uncertain.

JOSEPH. Hmmm.

ANNA.…It's sort of turning into a *UCAS* form, isn't it?

JOSEPH. What's his IQ?

ANNA.…I don't think he's got a very high IQ, Joe.

DAD. I told you. Too tall.

ANNA *clicks and scrolls.*

ANNA. Why do they all go on about *sport*? What is it about sport and sperm donors? Can't any of them read a book??

DAD. No. They're all wanking into cups.

JOSEPH (*reading off the screen*). 'My all-time favourite book is *The World According to Garp*.' Maybe Mum would be good to help choose…

ANNA. *Mum?* Why Mum? Mum thinks everyone is wonderful. Even when I was twenty-five and I had all the time in the world – you say I'm going out with Jugsy and I've found out he's a cokehead and he's been cheating on me and he's massively in debt and she says Anna are you sure you're not just being picky now?

DAD. She'd marry you off to a serial killer.

JOSEPH (*trills*). 'Mmm, he's so nice, he's got a beautiful cellar.'

DAD *gets up.*

DAD. Look. What about asking a real person. What about Nico? Intelligent, good-looking –

ANNA. Oh, God, Dad, no, not *Nico* – !!

DAD. Why not?

ANNA. He's so obviously fucked up.

DAD. I like him. He's a smoker.

JOSEPH. He's toxic!

ANNA. Complete philanderer, must be over fifty –

DAD. So what?

ANNA. Well I read that the sperms – the chances of autism and Asperger's, there's a link, over forty –

DAD. Bollocks! Are you saying my sperm wouldn't be up to it?

JOSEPH. Your sperm is dust, people could snort it.

DAD. I'm *always* trying to give my sperm out at cocktail parties. What are you saying, all my sperm have grey pubic hair, need a Stannah Stairlift?

ANNA. Just google it. There's a definite link.

...I mean, if anyone, I was thinking, what about Patrick?

DAD. *Patrick??* Christ, no! *Why?*

ANNA. Well, come on, Dad, he's a talented composer.

DAD. He's *not* a talented composer –

ANNA. The kid might be musical –

DAD. The kid will be bald! You can't do it with a bald man! I've seen Patrick without his top on. Seems to be tearing all that hair off his head and putting it on his back. Plus, he's *my* age! What about his autistic sperm?

JOSEPH. Worth it for the musical genes?

DAD. He could die tomorrow! Or he could carry on writing terrible operas for the next twenty years!

ANNA. But what they miss, these kids, is the *balance* of two parents. Even if we're *both* insane, we'll be insane in different ways –

DAD. Nah, and he's one of those puffy-eyed Scots – why would you do it with him?

ANNA (*firmly*). Well, I might not *have* to, because –
(*Brandishing laptop.*) this one *does* look really good. (*Sternly.*)
Why don't you actually look at these, Dad? It's *important*.
Look. Welsh German Israeli.

DAD. Sounds like a sheepdog.

DAD looks at the photo on the laptop screen skeptically.
Pause. He brightens.

…Hmmm! So this… *this* is…
A sperm donor?

ANNA. Yes.

DAD. Hmmmm!
…Well, he looks absolutely fine! Very handsome boy!
Lovely open face!
Brilliant! Go for it! Got a grin just like you, Joe.

JOSEPH. Thanks.

ANNA. Okay… but… okay…

She gets up.

Okay, suppose I do go with a sperm donor…
The thing is, I can't help wondering… it's all very convenient
for me, but I just keep wondering…
…How's the kid going to feel?

DAD. About what?

ANNA. About not having a dad.

DAD. They'll be absolutely fine!

ANNA. But the thing is…

She takes a breath.

I went online, when I first started thinking about this…

Beat.

And I found this *website*… and it's all these kids who were
conceived from anonymous sperm donors writing posts…
and some of them will never know who their dads are… and
others can only trace them after they turn eighteen… and
they're *fucking* angry.

JOSEPH. Angry with who?

ANNA. Angry with their mothers for conceiving them –

DAD. Oh fuck *off*.

ANNA. They have this huge angst because they don't know where half of them comes from –

DAD. Ah, grow up! This is all hysteria!

ANNA. But who knows, what would I have been like if I hadn't had a dad?

JOSEPH. Maybe you're fucked up because you *had* a dad. Him.

ANNA. That could be true, maybe *that's* why I've been out with a series of arseholes… but at least he's *here*…

DAD. For you to *blame*.

ANNA. *Anyway*… I have this *fear* that I'll give birth to this *angry* little girl –

JOSEPH. 'Genevieve' –

ANNA. – who will grow up to hate me because she doesn't know who she is, she'll be *angry* with me for depriving her of a father –

DAD (*hotly*). Well, if she is then you tell her to fuck off!

ANNA. *Dad* –

DAD. This is ridiculous. They're being unreasonable. *No one* asks to be born. Here I am, I'm sixty-nine, I didn't ask to be born –

ANNA. But it's obviously the way they feel!! Look. – *What* I think is, if I *have* to do it with an anonymous sperm donor, then I *will*, but I think first I'm going to have to at least *try* asking some actual men. Real men. If they will give me their sperm. – But *not* Nico.

Beat.

DAD. Not a good idea.

JOSEPH. / What??

ANNA. / You've just turned around a hundred and eighty degrees!

DAD (*airily*). Much cleaner, simpler to do it with a sperm donor. Do it with a real bloke, you'll have to deal with someone else's issues, demands, bullshit, neurosis, have to agree on a *name* together –

ANNA. But I thought you didn't *like* the idea of a sperm donor!!

DAD. But this one, what is he, Mr 21420, Nirvana fan, looks great. And it'll be *much* easier, simpler. Take it from me.

JOSEPH. You're the expert.

DAD. Well, that's what I think. Now – (*To* JOSEPH.) go and let Daisy out.

JOSEPH. Why me??

DAD. I want to watch the football.

JOSEPH. She's your fucking dog!

DAD. Don't be cruel. Poor old Daisy. Imagine being a dog, it must be hell. All the waiting around. Like being in the war. But they can't even smoke.

JOSEPH. Fucking hell.

He goes out.

ANNA. Well, thanks, anyway. For the advice.

DAD. No problem.

Beat.

I do find all this fascinating, Annie.

ANNA. Yeah?

DAD. Yes. It is incredible, this urge women have... a very clear, biological imperative... to sign up for, what is essentially, slavery... *willing* slavery, but slavery nonetheless...

ANNA. Mmm.

ANNA*'s* MOTHER *comes in, holding her laptop.*

DAD. Because *whatever* happens, it will be you, who will be looking after the baby… you know that… because Nature stacks the odds that way… I mean just look at women's *bodies*… hilariously basic… two thermos flasks and a rucksack… isn't that right, love?

MOTHER (*somewhat vaguely*). Oh, yes, absolutely… Is the wifi better in here do you think, I can't get anything in the study… Zach was trying to Skype me from New York…

Her laptop booms out the ringtone of Skype.

Oh there he is! (*Answering the Skype.*) Zach? Zach?

DAD. Christ. He's insatiable!

ZACH*'s voice comes from the laptop*

ZACH. *Mum? Can you hear me? You've frozen.*

MOTHER (*speaking over him*). Zach, can you hear me? You've frozen. (*Speaking loudly.*) I'm going upstairs where the reception is better.

She goes out.

DAD. Fucking hell. He was just on the Skype to *me*! For an *hour*. Telling me the plot of the film he'd just seen, minute by minute. I might as well have *watched* it.

ANNA. He's lonely. He's just broken up with his boyfriend.

Beat.

DAD. Listen, Pips. Listen to me. It's not a tragedy if you don't have one. It's important to realise that. It's not a tragedy that Tom left you.

Beat.

Having a child who dies when they're four – *that's* a tragedy. You've got to understand… Having a child feels like exposing yourself to *risk*.

Anything can happen to them before they're forty.

And just when you think you can *stop* worrying about them, *they* turn forty. And *they* start worrying. That *they* haven't had a child.

You don't ever stop worrying.

Love is worry.

Scene Three

38

A bedroom. ANNA and TOM face each other. TOM is distraught, weeping. He is in shorts and trainers – running gear.

ANNA. Right…

TOM. I just feel like… I've been feeling really unsure… and it's getting… I can't ignore it any more…

ANNA. I see…

TOM. I feel like… I'm… heading for some great unhappiness…

He starts to weep again in great sobs.

ANNA. But maybe that's because… you… you're making a mistake… *right now*… maybe *that's* the great unhappiness…

TOM. All I know is that I don't… I mean I was crying when we went to the hospital… I'm crying now…

ANNA. I know…

TOM. I just don't feel sure enough…

ANNA. But Tom, we've made the… we've *made* them now…

TOM. I know…

ANNA. I can't just… throw the embryos away… tomorrow is when they put them in…

TOM. I know…

ANNA. What do you want to happen?

TOM. I don't know...

ANNA. I mean, Tom, honestly, I don't think anyone *ever* feels
    sure, especially not men... my dad, I told my dad that you
    were having doubts and he *sympathises,* he never wanted kids,
    I was a mistake, he was deeply depressed, but once they *had*
    me, he completely turned around, you won't feel sure until the
    baby is out, that's perfectly natural and normal –

TOM. I don't want to *do* it not feeling sure.

ANNA. I don't think men *ever* feel sure, Tom, believe me...

TOM. It can't be right if I feel *this* scared, I have to listen to the
    way I'm feeling...

ANNA. But Tom, you're talking like we're about to commit a
    murder or do something *evil,* all we're doing is trying to
    make a baby, we've been trying for *two years* and you've
    been fine, I think it was just the hospital and the fact that it
    was all suddenly so medicalised, the NHS, of course it's
    going to feel unnatural and weird –

TOM. No, when we had to talk to that doctor, I felt he was
    looking right into me, he *knew* I wasn't sure and I just felt
    like 'He's right', he looked right into my soul and saw me
    for the faker I was.

    Beat.

    I haven't been fine. I've been having doubts for a while now,
    and I don't think I should ignore them any more.

    Beat.

    I just think, what if, okay, we're all right now, but what if
    we're happy for ten years and then I leave you?

ANNA.... Well, that could happen, I can't promise to you it
    wouldn't happen, no one gets a guarantee.

TOM. Isn't it more of a cruelty to leave you and a child after ten
    years than to listen to my doubts now?

    Beat.

ANNA. Not necessarily…

Pause.

TOM. Sometimes…

…I look at you…

…and I wonder 'Is Anna looking older today?'

Beat. ANNA *is winded by this.*

ANNA. Right…

Beat.

The thing is… I *will* get older. I *will* look older. There's kind of nothing I can do about that.

(*Somewhat sharply.*) And I know there's a big age gap between us, but actually, *you* will get older as well.

TOM.…And I think about other women. I look at other women on the street and I find them attractive.

ANNA. But Tom, that's completely normal, for fuck's sake!

TOM. I didn't when we were first going out.

ANNA. But that's the way it *works*! You start off –

TOM. I think if I really felt enough for you I wouldn't be thinking about other women.

Beat.

What if I want to sleep with someone else?

ANNA. Well… people… do end up sleeping with other people.

Beat.

I would fucking deal with it. You can't have a relationship for years and years and years and things *not* happen.

TOM. Yes you can. Look at my parents. They've been married for decades, neither of them has done anything. Their relationship is perfect, in fact it's intimidating to me how perfect it is –

ANNA. For fuck's sake, that's because your parents present you with a *Disney* idea of… I'm… okay, I don't want to slag off your parents.

Beat.

Look, if it makes you feel less panicky… obviously, I wouldn't *want* you to, I would hate it, but if you did sleep with someone else, I'd like to think it wouldn't be the… I'd try to deal with it. It wouldn't be the end of the world. Would that make you feel less trapped?

You could sleep with someone else if you wanted to.

Beat.

TOM. Yeah, I don't want that kind of bohemian thing. *Your* parents, they… but I don't want that – compromised thing.

ANNA *explodes in frustration.*

ANNA. God, Tom, don't you realise how *rare* it is to find someone who makes you laugh, who your brain connects with, you fancy, who doesn't *bore* you?? It took me twenty years to find you! It terrifies me because you *will* find out and it will be *too late,* that it's not just me, you will *always* notice other women, whoever you're with, it is *human nature* – you just don't realise because you're too *young* –

TOM *has started to well up during this.*

TOM. But –

ANNA. And you can write ten thousand narratives about what *might* happen! Yes, you might leave me in ten years, or twenty, or – it's all *hypothetical* but this, now, is *real* –

TOM *(tearfully, bewildered).*…. How can you be so strong? How can you be so sure?

ANNA. Because I've had a thousand shit relationships! I *did* the sleeping with people, in my twenties, it was a waste of time, I would gladly have skipped that whole decade, early thirties too, please, take it from me, you are missing *nothing* –

TOM. *But I can't use your experience!* You tell me all that again and again, it doesn't help me, I can't *know* it or believe it just from listening what happened to you. I have to live it, I have to know it for *myself*.

Beat.

I have to... I think I have to go... I have to leave...

He wells up again.

ANNA.... You're in your running gear...

TOM *hugs her, bursts into fresh sobs.*

TOM. Oh my God... I can't believe I'm doing this... I love you so much...

(*Into her shoulder.*) I have to go...

He weeps.

You've taught me everything... You're everything to me... I love you so much...

Comes away from her, still weeping, looks at her, bewildered.

If only I always felt this intensely about you. Then I'd be sure.

He leaves.

Scene Four

38

ANNA *sits on a bed with a little* GIRL, *sifting through a pile of children's books that the little* GIRL *has brought her.*

ANNA. Okay, so shall I read to you or shall I make one up?

GIRL. Make one up.

ANNA. Yes. Why don't we start by reading one and that'll give me time to make one up.

GIRL. No.

Beat.

ANNA. This one?

GIRL. No.

ANNA. What about –

GIRL. No.

ANNA. Well, let's just start by reading one… to give me time, okay, to *think* of a story, yeah, because this one looks *great*… and *then* I'll make one up for you. Okay?

And you do your teeth when I'm reading it. Here.

She gives the little GIRL *her toothbrush, squirting a bit of toothpaste on it.*

Mmmm… Strawberry toothpaste!

She settles herself with the book.

'*Are You My Mother?*'

The GIRL *curls up next to her on the bed with the toothbrush in her mouth like a lollipop stick.*

'A mother bird sat on her egg.
The egg jumped.
"Oh oh!" said the mother bird. "My baby" – '

GIRL. No, it's 'Uh-oh.' '*Uh-oh.*'

Beat.

ANNA. Right. '"My baby will be here! He will want to eat."'

GIRL. You didn't say it. 'Uh-oh'.

ANNA. Well, I'm just making it up a bit, aren't I. Like you wanted.

ANNA turns a page.

'So away she went.
The egg jumped. It jumped, and jumped, and jumped!
Out came the baby bird!'

GIRL. This is your room now.

ANNA.... Yes, I suppose it is.

GIRL (*stretching out her arms*). I like stretching my arms.

ANNA.... Yes.

She carries on reading.

'"Where is my mother?" said the baby bird.'

GIRL. This is from when I was *little*.

ANNA. '...He did not know what his mother looked like. He came to a kitten. "Are you my mother?" he said to the' –

GIRL. *Why* are you staying with us?

ANNA. Well, because I'm... between places at the moment.

GIRL. We bought this house in 2006. This is *our* spare room. My daddy buyed the bed.

ANNA. I know.
'The kitten and the hen were not his mother. Did he have a mother? "I did have a mother," said the baby bird. – "I" – '

GIRL. Silly.

ANNA. '"I know I did. I have to find her. I will. I WILL!"'

The little GIRL forcibly closes the book.

Oh dear. We didn't even finish it.

GIRL. Make up a story. A scary story.

ANNA.... Hm, okay, well, what story shall I tell you?

GIRL (*a fact*). There's water in the air and you can't see it.

ANNA. Yes. Even in this room there's water in the air.

GIRL. Some buried treasure floats.

ANNA. Does it!

GIRL. How do you know Mummy?

ANNA. Ah, well, Mummy is my friend and we were at school together. And when I first moved to London the first person I lived with was your mummy *and* an old old lady called Natasha and she was Russian.

GIRL. Why was she rushing?

ANNA. Well, because –

GIRL. Because she was late?

ANNA. *Because* she'd come here from Russia.

GIRL. Why?

ANNA. Because she was Jewish and the Nazis – erm, because of the war. And this big old house belonged to Natasha and we lived up on the top floor and there were *no radiators*. So we got very very cold. And this old lady Natasha spoke with a Russian accent –

GIRL. Is this my story?

ANNA. Yes.

GIRL. But you're not making it up.

ANNA. Well, I am and I'm not.

GIRL. You're not.

ANNA. But that's the best kind of story. Because it's interesting... because you know it's true.

GIRL. Why is that interesting?

ANNA. I don't know. Anyway Natasha had a poodle. And one day the poodle was cross about something and he came up to our floor and... he did a pee and poo where he wasn't supposed to!

GIRL. Where?!

ANNA. Well, he got up on to our landing and first he did a poo there...

GIRL. A poo?!

The little GIRL *covers her mouth with her hands, stands up, wobbling, on the bed.*

ANNA. And your mummy had all her shoes out in a row, you know the way she does, and he pee'd on *all* your mummy's best high-heeled shoes!!

The GIRL *shrieks with laughter, starts to jump up and down on the bed.*

GIRL. What – did – Mummy – *do*?!

ANNA. She tried to wash them. Actually she moved out quite soon after that because she met Daddy. Sweetie, don't jump up and down –

GIRL. But – I – like – it – !

ANNA. Stop it or I won't be able to tell the story –

The GIRL *slowly stops bouncing.*

...And... After that every time someone came to stay the night with me the dog would bark when they went up the stairs.

GIRL. Who stayed the night?

ANNA....Friends and things.

Beat.

GIRL. It always rains on me because I'm lucky.

The GIRL *starts to gently bounce again.*

ANNA. Mm... that's a good way to look at it. No bouncing.

The bouncing persists.

GIRL. I want something nice to eat...

ANNA. Not now. In the morning.

She looks at her watch.

…Aren't you tired yet?

The GIRL *stops bouncing, gradually, but remains standing.*

GIRL. But what happened next?

Beat.

ANNA. Um. Well. Well, she got older and older.

GIRL. Who?

ANNA. The old lady Natasha. And she'd fall in the night and I'd wake up because she'd be shouting for help. And I'd have to go down and try to pick her up… and she was really heavy…

The GIRL *sits back down, interested.*

GIRL. Heavier than me?

ANNA. Much heavier. And one day she fell and they took her into hospital and I visited her there and all she would eat was apple puree and then not even that any more and then… She died. With her chin resting on her hand, like this. Poor Natasha.

Beat.

She didn't have any children.

GIRL. Why?

ANNA. I think… because of… what happened to her relatives in the war. She thought she didn't want to.

Pause. The GIRL *lies on her back, still, looks up at the ceiling.*

GIRL. What happens next?

ANNA. I don't know.

Beat.

GIRL. What would happen if you smacked the sun?

Scene Five

38

ANNA *and* TOM *sit in a café.* TOM *is breezy and cheerful.*

TOM. It's lovely to see you. You look *really* well.

ANNA. Thanks.

TOM. How's the casting! I want to hear all about it!

ANNA. Oh it's a nightmare. As always. We're going to have to think out of the box. Go a bit older, or... And the *doubling* is really tricky... do I get the mother to be played by the same actress, or what... I really don't think we're going to be cast in time... it's terrifying...

TOM *laughs, pours her some tea.*

TOM. You're looking great.

ANNA. Thanks... I'm staying with Beth at the moment, her kids wake up so early... It's brilliant, Nutella and peanut butter every day for breakfast...

Beat. TOM *puts his hand on her hand.*

TOM. It is so great to see you.

ANNA. Yeah...

Pause.

So, your mum must be relieved.

Beat.

That the IVF didn't work.

Beat.

TOM. Well. I told them both they would just have to get on with it if it *did* work.

ANNA. The day you left, she wrote me an email begging me not to put in the embryos. For your sake, for the unborn child's sake, and for my sake. I thought that was fabulous – for *my* sake.

TOM *puts his head in his hands.*

TOM. I can't believe she did that. I was so angry.
    She's a fucking bitch…

    Beat.

    It's actually made me really question things… my family…
    I've never really challenged them before.

ANNA. Yup.

    TOM *gets a little tearful.*

TOM. You've, when you've, behaved so well… and then she,
    she does *that*…

    Beat.

ANNA. Well.

    She's your mother.

    Pause.

    So, I thought we should meet, now, you know, a bit of time's
    passed…

TOM. Yeah, I'm really glad you called, it's great to see you.

ANNA.…Now that you've had time to think how you feel,
    I wanted to see how you're feeling… now.

TOM. Yeah.

    Beat.

ANNA. So how – I've just been trying to give you space.

TOM. Yeah.

    Beat.

ANNA. How are you?

TOM. Yeah, well, it's good actually. Henry and I are going to be
    moving in together –

ANNA. Oh, right.

TOM. – the flats Dad bought us are ready, so yeah, we're going
    to be living in one together and we're renting out the one
    below to help pay the mortgage.

ANNA. Right. That's nice.

TOM. It has been really nice actually, living with Hen again, getting to know him again. It's been really nice. I've been writing *loads*...

ANNA. Mhmm, mhm. Right. Great.

TOM. I don't really like the way Mum's done up the flats, but you know, you can't really stop her...

ANNA. No. You can't.

Beat.

Well, I wanted to see you because I need to know what you're thinking.
About what happened. And, you know.
Now.

TOM. Right.

Beat.

I don't think I've made a mistake.

Beat.

ANNA. Okay.

Beat.

TOM. Yeah, I've thought about it a lot, of course, and obviously I miss you, Annie, I miss so many things... being able to tell you stuff as soon it happens, like that grim camping trip with Robin –

ANNA. Well, you *did* ring me when it –

TOM. Or you know I've been reading Noël Coward and of course it's *you* I want to talk to about it straight away, about how brilliant he is, and every time I see a shit play, and I miss all our in-jokes,
– but I don't think I've made a mistake.

ANNA. Right.

Pause.

The thing is, Tom, what worries me is that I think you're very very good at burying things... you went to boarding school and I think you're capable of forcing yourself to live life on a very superficial level where you don't allow yourself to feel all the painful shit for months and months and months. But it doesn't mean it goes away. It will come out. And I think you'll get a massive shock when it does.

TOM. Mm. But… I don't think I've made a mistake.

Beat.

I don't think I should have a baby with you.

Beat.

ANNA. Okay, I have a feeling that what's going to happen to you is you'll go back to living a very conventional life and everyone will tell you that you did the right thing because it's not conventional for a twenty-six-year-old man to have a baby with a thirty-eight-year-old woman. There aren't any examples around to tell you it's okay. All you see is your twenty-year-old friends and your parents and your parents are very conventional and you're pressurised by your parents and their expectations –

TOM. I'm not.

Beat.

My parents would support me in whatever I wanted to do if I was sure I wanted to do it.
But I'm *not* sure.

Beat.

I was feeling a huge pressure. I felt really under pressure.
I feel better now.
I don't want responsibilities like that. At this point. I want to be freer. I know that now.

Beat. During ANNA*'s next speech* TOM *becomes tearful.*

ANNA. You sort of… yeah, you're sort of… it's like… Tom,

Sorry, I…

It's like, I worry I did the wrong thing, letting you go and have 'space', because you're already different, you sound… fake. Sort of stiff and formal and *wooden*. It's like you've been telling yourself a *story* until you believe it and you've built up this protective, fake, *shell* around yourself –

TOM. I think I've made the right decision.

ANNA. And this story you're telling yourself, I worry any time you start doubting your decision, you'll just tell it to yourself again and there won't be anyone to tell you that your story is a lie, you're lying to yourself. And you'll carry on the rest of your life with this lie, and that will be it.

Beat.

TOM. I don't think I'm lying to myself.

ANNA. We were trying for *two years.*

TOM. I know but I don't think I was being honest with myself.

ANNA. You weren't being honest with yourself, now you aren't lying to yourself – Which is which?

I don't think you know who you are.

Beat.

I actually *worry* about you because I'll have to go out there, I can't mess about, I'll be thirty-nine in a month, I'll have to do it with someone else and that could happen very very soon and how will you *feel*?
I think you'll feel shit.

Beat.

TOM. I don't know.

Pause.

ANNA. What about if I just asked you for your sperm? Would that be better for you?

Pause.

TOM. No.

I don't want to do that.

Beat.

ANNA. Okay, well, what if I asked someone *else* for their sperm and had a baby with them, and *then* we got back together?

TOM *looks very uncomfortable. Pause.*

TOM. I...
   I hadn't really thought about that.
   ...I suppose I could think about it...

   Beat. With flat certainty.

   I don't think I would want to do that.

ANNA. ...What *do* you want?

   What are you feeling?

TOM. I feel... stupid.
   I feel silly for not having realised sooner.

ANNA. Realised what?

TOM. How I felt.

   Pause.

ANNA. You know, Tom, I haven't said so many things to you,
   I've been trying so hard not to pressure you. Thirty-six to
   thirty-nine are quite crucial years –

TOM (*carefully*). I don't think it's my fault you chose to go out
   with me for those years. I don't think it's my fault you were
   thirty-six when I met you.

ANNA. For fuck's sake, Tom, you sound like a fucking
   barrister! If I'd got pregnant at the beginning – but you had
   time to start questioning your feelings like picking and
   picking a hole in a sweater and did you feel enough for me
   but frankly it's an impossible test, the *only* person we carry
   on feeling intensely about forever is *ourselves*!

TOM. When we got together, it was you that rang me up. You
   always knew what you wanted. I feel like I never made the
   choice.

ANNA. How do you think it felt near the end, having sex and
   then you pulling out every time you wanted to come,
   sticking your cock in my mouth instead? Have you any idea
   how hurtful that was?
   And when you kept going on about whether it would be
   more cruel to leave me now, or ten years later with a kid?

I tell you what's cruel. To do what you're doing now. To leave me with nothing.

TOM *is crying again.*

I went out with you because I thought you were such a special person. I still think that what we had was special and real.
And would last forever. You obviously don't feel that's true. We'll just have to see which of us turns out to be wrong.

Pause.

TOM. I don't think I've made a mistake.

Beat.

ANNA. Okay, well, I don't think I can have any more contact with you.

Beat.

TOM.... Right.

ANNA. No more phone calls, no more emails. Because I don't think you really know what it is to lose me.

Beat. TOM *is visibly surprised and shaken. His voice falters.*

TOM.... Well, if that's what you want, then...

I have to respect that.

Pause. He starts to get up. Uncertainly –

Okay.

I suppose, I'll, if I made a mistake, then.
I'll be in touch.

He leaves.

Scene Six

39

The middle of the night. ANNA is standing in her pyjamas, hair messy, no make-up, in tears. JOSEPH stands watching her, in his pyjama bottoms, looking frightened. ANNA finally manages to speak through her sobs.

ANNA. I'm *frightened...*

JOSEPH. It'll be okay...

ANNA sobs a bit more.

ANNA. Joe...

JOSEPH. What's wrong...

ANNA. Joe... I don't know if I believe in God any more...

JOSEPH. Right... great...

He looks at his watch, rubs his eyes.

Wow it's really late... have you been to sleep?

She tries to breathe.

ANNA. ...No, couldn't sleep, just been lying there, and then I just... I had this horrible...

JOSEPH. Okay...

ANNA. I don't even want to say it...

JOSEPH. It's okay, tell me...
I am, I'm awake now...

She gulps.

ANNA. I don't know how to describe it...
Joe, I've always comforted myself with the thought that there's a *reason* that stuff happens, that it's all part of some plan, it's just a necessary part of... Do you know what I mean?

JOSEPH. Yep, yep... uh-huh...

ANNA. That there's some kind of point to it all... you know?

He nods.

...So all the crap men I went out with, they were part of the story leading up to me meeting Tom... it all made sense... But I was lying there in the dark thinking, and I suddenly got really scared, because I know, I *know*, that if I'd only got pregnant with Tom, it would all have been okay.

Beat.

JOSEPH. Well... yeah...

ANNA. I'm not talking bollocks. Am I?

Beat.

JOSEPH. No... You're not... I think you're right... I think he would have been okay.

ANNA. Even *Dad* said, when he left me in the middle of IVF, stay calm, wait and see if you're pregnant... If you're pregnant Tom will come round –

JOSEPH. Yeah.

ANNA. – But I *didn't* get pregnant... my fucking body let me down...

JOSEPH. He could still come back...

ANNA. Joe... I don't think he's going to come back...

She starts crying again.

And this time, I can't see *why*... I can't find a reason... I mean why the IVF needed to fail... Tom has left me... I'm thirty-nine... I'm childless... I'm going to die without children – only *bad* has come out of this...

And I thought. That's because there *is* no grand plan. There's no one watching the story. It's all just random. The universe is huge and pointless and random...

JOSEPH. Okay... well...

ANNA. And *pitiless*... And Joe, that scares me... I can't see a way out...!!

JOSEPH. Okay look... shhh... shh...

ANNA. No, suddenly nothing makes sense... Am I doing the wrong thing? Cutting contact with Tom? Am I making a mistake? There's no *reason* for anything any more – there's no God –

JOSEPH. I don't think you're making a mistake – I don't think you're making a mistake.

ANNA. But how do you know?

JOSEPH. Okay, okay, shhh. Let's not worry about the universe or God for the moment, let's –

When you kept contact with him he got his shit together and said thanks very much but he didn't want to have a baby with you, it didn't *work*. You've tried it with the door open, now try it with the door closed.

Beat.

By not having contact with him you're saving yourself all those daily small jealousies and miseries – it was driving you *nuts*, when he called, when he didn't call, with his stupid Sloaney life, whenever he felt like offloading or talking about some fucking Ken *Tynan* letter he'd been reading or – I'm not having this actually, he's a fucking cunt!

ANNA (*obliviously, lost*). The thought is so large... so dark... I don't know what to do with it... if this doesn't make sense... then nothing makes sense... there's no point in anything...

JOSEPH. Okay, you're still thinking about the universe. *If* he was too weak to go through IVF then you have to think he's not the right person for you. You –

ANNA. But that's *it*, that's what I've been doing, imposing a coherent *narrative* on it, I don't think there is one. What if he *is* right for me, but the wrong thing happened. And in another world where the IVF worked we would have been fine.

Then what's happened is – there's nothing to redeem it – it's just... a disaster...

She cries.

JOSEPH. Pips… Pippy…

He hugs her.

I'm going to get you a glass of milk. And a banana.

He goes out. ANNA, *alone, sits on the bed. Puts her face in her hands, briefly cries. Stops. Dries her eyes. Stares into space.* JOE *comes back in with a glass of milk, gives it to her.*

ANNA. Why do I keep fucking up with men? Why does this keep happening?

JOSEPH. You've had a lot of bad luck.

ANNA. Maybe it's not bad luck. I've chosen them all. Maybe I've chosen my bad luck.

JOSEPH. Some of them chose you.

ANNA. And I let them.

Beat.

I really regret having gone out with Julian. There's nothing redeeming about that time.

JOSEPH. 'Jugsy.'

ANNA. Yeah, 'Jugsy'. What a waste of my twenties.

JOSEPH. It's not your fault he was a cunt.

ANNA. But I knew he was, deep down.

JOSEPH. No you didn't. It's not like you've got like a metal detector at the airport… that goes beep beep beep bastard… you *have* to go out with people a bit to find out if they're a cunt.

ANNA. Maybe I've just got a narrative in my head that things will never work out with anyone and so they *don't*, it's a self-fulfilling prophecy, it's my fault –

JOSEPH. Okay hang on, you just said you were scared because there *was* no narrative, now you're inventing yourself a *negative* one –

ANNA. I'm just trying find a *reason*! Even if it's *me*! I'm
scared and I don't understand why this keeps happening –
it's like *Groundhog* Day.

Beat.

Maybe I should do therapy.

Beat.

Beth sees a Lacanian therapist. Who talks about her inner
child.

JOSEPH. Well, it's fucking dark.
Up your own arse.

ANNA *laughs weakly.*

We will look on a website. You can meet and ask people.
You can make a list. You will be okay.

Beat.

And about God… if he does exist, Pips… I don't think he's
the plot.
I think that he's the lighting.

ANNA.…I'm just worried… I have no – I don't know what
happens next.

Beat.

I have to decide what's going to *happen* to me.

They look at each other.

Scene Seven

39 + 1

ANNA *and* LACHLAN *sit together in a café.* LACHLAN *is Irish. Initially* ANNA *is extremely bright and cheerful.* LACHLAN *is also very warm.*

ANNA. So, my God! When did we last...

LACHLAN. It was that reading... wasn't it? Yeah, must have been...

ANNA. *Five* years ago? God!

LACHLAN.... Yeah... Wow...! I really really liked that script you know, *I* thought it was amazing... I thought he was a great writer...

ANNA. Yeah well... That's life...

LACHLAN. But it was *such* a good day, you got such a good feeling in the room going, Anna...

ANNA. Oh thanks, thanks... But what have *you* been doing?

LACHLAN (*a touch of weariness*). Oh... I did that series... I thought it was going to be really interesting, way more interesting than it actually turned out... and...

ANNA. About superpowers?

LACHLAN. Sort of... aliens... anyway... it's done now. I can stop working out. Thank God. And... I'm just reading this...

He gestures.

Anna Karenina... cos they want to see me for Levin...?

ANNA. Oh wow! Oh, I *love* that character, that's an amazing part... *And* you wouldn't have to work out, he's a fattie...

LACHLAN. – Yeah...!

ANNA. Gosh well best of luck... I should really re-read it...

Yeah...

Yeah...

Erm…

Yeah…

So, Lachlan –

I know this is a bit out of the blue…

LACHLAN. No, no, it's lovely to see you, I'm really glad you called.

ANNA. But erm, I'm, um…

To her surprise she is suddenly close to tears but the voice and words that come out are oddly formal.

Erm, I've come to a time in my life when,
erm, I realise that I really want children, well, a child, and,
um, the thing is I'm nearly forty, and I'm in a situation where I'm single,
and so, I'm, having to think of a different way to do it,
and I thought of you.

Beat. She can't hold in the tears any longer.

Sorry… sorry… I'm sorry…

She cries for a few seconds

LACHLAN.…No no, it's… fine…

She manages to regain control and continues.

ANNA.…I have no idea if you're single or not, or what's going on in your life, but I've always really liked you although I don't know you particularly well. And, I just thought I would ask in case it might be something… you might… be…

Her voice has started to shake and she has to stop again.

Sorry…

LACHLAN. No really, Anna, it's fine…

ANNA. You've just always seemed so nice, and I've been trying to think who to ask and I don't know why but you came into my head and so I thought the only way would be to ask. I know it sounds crazy.

LACHLAN. No, I understand, I understand.

ANNA. It sounds crazy.

LACHLAN. It doesn't, it doesn't sound crazy at all.

ANNA.... Sorry, I don't know why I keep *crying*... It's all a bit intense for a Wednesday afternoon... something about having to say it all out loud... I didn't know it would be so... You're the first person I've asked.

LACHLAN. No, I really respect you for asking. It's a very brave thing to ask.

Beat.

And actually, Anna, you know, I *do* understand, cos, in many ways, you're right. It *is* something I should be thinking about.

Beat.

This has been a weird year. I am single actually. I broke up with my girlfriend, I really thought she was the one – I don't know what it is, but anyway, I always seem to go out with people who lie.

Anyway, we broke up, and the other thing that happened this year is that my sister died.

ANNA. Oh my *God*, I'm so sorry!

LACHLAN. It's okay.

ANNA. I had no *idea*.

LACHLAN. It's fine, I haven't talked to many people about it. I've been waiting for it to happen in many ways.

ANNA. What – was she –

LACHLAN. She committed suicide.

ANNA.... Oh my God...

LACHLAN. It's okay, I've always, for a long time now, we lived together, I always dreaded, you know, that one day I would walk in on her... anyway yeah, it was me that found the body.

ANNA. Oh, Lachlan, my God, I can't imagine what that must have been like...

LACHLAN. Well.

Beat.

It wasn't quite clear if she... we don't really know if it was suicide, she might have OD'd by mistake.
It's okay, I'm much better than I was.

ANNA. I can't... um... Lachlan, how awful... I just... can't... I mean the only...

Beat.

The only thing I can think to say is that, um, my mum said it helped, seeing her mum's body when she died, but of course that was completely different.

Um because, she could see that the spirit wasn't there any more in the body. And the fact that she could see that it was separate to the body made her realise the spirit might live on. She says she felt her mum's spirit around her for weeks afterwards. Um, in the house.

Beat.

LACHLAN. Well, what I know from seeing her body is there is no life after death. That's what I knew when I saw it. For sure.

There wasn't anything positive to understand from it.

Silence.

ANNA. I'm so sorry.

LACHLAN. No... it's...

Beat.

I'm just beginning to come out the other side.

Silence.

...But,
...it did make me think – a lot – about... *my* life, and, so, I understand your whole – how you must be feeling.

ANNA. Christ, I mean – my – !
   It's – forget I ever –
   I really don't want to pile more onto your plate…
   shoulders…

LACHLAN. No, Anna.

ANNA. I feel embarrassed for even mentioning it now.

LACHLAN. No, don't. Don't.

   Pause.

   Listen, Anna, I think maybe what we should do, is hang out
   and see each other again and just get to know each other a bit
   better.

   Beat.

   Maybe, go to the cinema or a gallery or something. And just
   see what happens.

   Beat.

ANNA. Wow, Lachlan.
   Really?
   Thank you so much for not – not just dismissing it.

LACHLAN. No. It was a brave thing for you to ask.

   Beat. He starts to get up. Smiles.

   You know, as I was walking here, I wondered why you
   wanted to see me.

   Beat.

   I thought you were going to offer me a part.

Scene Eight

39 + 2

The little GIRL *lies quietly in bed,* ANNA *sits reading aloud to her.*

ANNA. 'What good luck!
Ned got a letter that said,
"Please come to a surprise party."
What bad luck!
The party was in Florida and he was in New York.
What good luck!
A friend lent him an airplane.
What bad luck!
The motor exploded…'

The little GIRL *has fallen asleep but* ANNA *reads on. Fade.*

Scene Nine

39 + 3

ANNA *sits in a café with* DANNY. DANNY *is South London and a bit 'street' in his mannerisms, he is tucking in to a plate of food.*

DANNY. Nah nah, I'm vegetarian – you didn't *know* that?!

ANNA. No!

DANNY. For years, man! Yeah, when I went to Argentina, mate, I tasted the beef there and I was like, if that is what beef is supposed to taste like, I ain't eating *our* shit no more. No hardship believe me, to give it up.

ANNA.…Don't you get a bit – anaemic?

DANNY. Not at all, darling, not at all. No. You don't need it, I'm telling you, you don't need it, it's a big con. Make yourself a nice green juice in the morning, you're set up for the day –

ANNA. How's the music?

DANNY. It's okay, it's okay, it's just keeping going with everything else, you know what I mean? Three gigs last weekend, by Sunday I was on the sofa, had to knock out a few zeds – five hours later –

His phone rings, he picks it up.

Hey.

Yeah well it depends on Kush.
Well look, mate, lemme see if Kush is available.
All right.
Laters. I'm with a gorgeous friend here so I've got to go.

ANNA *smirks weakly. He puts the phone down.*

We've got an amazing line-up, you should come check it out, next Saturday. Kush, Son Yambu, Baba Suvaku – you should come!

ANNA. I will, I will.

DANNY. But, bubba, how are *you* doing, I want to know what's going on in Anna world, it's been too long!

ANNA. Yeah! Well…

DANNY. Cos we keep playing telephone tennis, babe, I'm sorry about that, fucking mad, first there were the gigs, also I've been trying to sell my flat –

ANNA. Oh no! How's that going?

DANNY. Well, you know how it is, you know how it is. But how are you?

ANNA. Well –

DANNY. People say they're going to buy it, then they say they're not going to buy it, la la la. And there's a bit of a time pressure cos after this I'm off to LA, yeah I'm doing what my manager tells me to at last, so I'm really glad we managed to hook up – but how are you, babe?

ANNA. Okay well listen, Danny, the reason I kept calling you is a bit of a weird one and like I said, I didn't really want to ask you about it over the phone –

DANNY. No that's right, that's right, you did say that, so yeah, Anna, I'll be honest, I did wonder –

ANNA. Okay. So. Danny. Just listen a sec.

Beat.

The thing is, Danny,
I need to have a baby. And, erm, you're a very talented guy and –

DANNY. Ohhhh! – You want me to be your *babyfather*!!

Beat. ANNA *is a bit taken aback.*

ANNA. Well… Yeah. (You got there quite fast…)

DANNY. That's very interesting, that's very interesting.

ANNA. Um because –

DANNY. Why did you think of me?

Beat.

ANNA. Well –

DANNY. Cos interestingly, interestingly, someone asked me about that before, yeah years ago, this girl. I said no.
But you know it's very interesting, why did you think of me?

Beat.

ANNA. Well, Danny, I suppose I think you're very talented, you're very, you know, talented, and I think it would be a good mix. We would make an amazing kid.

You're the first person I've asked.

He preens slightly.

The first person I thought of.
I haven't asked anyone else.

DANNY. Hmm. Hmmm. Hmmmm.
I'll be honest. It's interesting. You've interested me, Anna, because this is fucking *real*, you know what I mean? You've asked me something *real*.

ANNA. Well, thanks.

He pushes the food around his plate for a moment, thinking.

DANNY....But is it romantic, is that what you're saying?

ANNA. No, no, that's not what I'm asking.

DANNY. Because *we* had that thing...

ANNA. Yeah I know, but I thought I'd just take that out of the equation.

DANNY. No but you want the whole package, don't you.

ANNA. No, no, I don't. I'm just asking –

DANNY. No but you do. I'm not talking about me. Be honest now. In an ideal world, I'm not saying with *me*, but you want to be with someone, don't you, and be a family.

ANNA. Well in the end I want to end up with someone but that's not what I'm asking you for.

DANNY. Okay but let's just talk about this.

Beat.

Don't you think a kid needs a full-on dad?

ANNA....Well I suppose in an ideal world, yes, but there are so many ways to –

DANNY. No no no but listen. Don't *you* want a full-on dad for the kid.

ANNA. Honestly, it's whatever you would want it to be.

DANNY. But I dunno, the thing is, *I* think a kid needs a full-on dad, I think if you're going to do it, if I was going to do it, I *should* be a full-on dad, otherwise it's not fair on the kid. That's the way it should be.

ANNA. But Danny, if that's what you feel, then I don't have a problem with that, that's *good*. That's great!

DANNY. Aha, you see, that's what you really *want*, isn't it!!

Beat.

ANNA. What?

DANNY. That's what you really *want* deep down, Anna! A full-on dad!

ANNA. Erm –

DANNY. – And the thing is I don't feel I can do that.

Beat.

ANNA. Oh.

DANNY. No, no no.

ANNA. Right. – But I'm not asking –

DANNY. No, I don't want to do that. Not at the moment. In fact I don't know if I could *ever* do that.

ANNA. Okay… Well… what about if you weren't – a full-on –

DANNY. No, I see where you're going with this Anna, and no, because a dad *should* be full-on. I don't think it's right to be any other way.

ANNA. Okay…

DANNY. But *I* can't commit to doing full-on. I can't commit to that. No.

ANNA. Riiight…

Beat.

(*Drily.*) You know that's pretty *watertight* logic you've got going there, Danny, isn't it.

But DANNY *is in his own thoughts.*

DANNY (*dreamily*)….It's weird because I know I've got to have kids and settle down one day but it's a bit like going to the dentist. I know I've got to *do* it but…

ANNA. You don't really want to?

DANNY. Yeah…

Beat.

But you know what, at least you're fucking real, Anna. At least you're asking me something fucking real.

I tell you what, bubba, I'll think about it. I'll really think about it.

Beat.

Do you want to get a drink?

Scene Ten

39 + 4

ANNA *stands in a beautiful apartment with* CORIN.

CORIN....Here... it's actually Chinese...

He pours her some tea from a beautiful cast-iron pot.

ANNA. Oh look at that pot...!

She looks around

It's so beautiful here...

CORIN. Well, yes I'll show you the other floors in a minute – no I'm not sure how long you're meant to brew it for...

He peers at the tea.

I got it when I was filming with Woody...

ANNA. Oh really...!
...How *was* he?

CORIN. Wonderful. A real pleasure to direct.

ANNA. You didn't ever disagree?

CORIN. No, no...

Only *once*... Silly really... it was a scene that I felt, well, you know his *humour*, very improvised, but there was *one* scene, you know, about the Holocaust...

ANNA. Oh... yes...?

CORIN. I felt it needed to be played without all that…
zaniness… and improvised silly small talk, and there we
were trying to do it again and again… and it just felt so
horribly phoney. And fake… and I had to stop and I said I I I
just can't do this; can you please just play the scene. Cut all
those jokes, cut right to the chase really. To his credit,
Woody backed right off and just played the scene.

ANNA. Great.

Beat.

CORIN. Mmm. Yes.

Pause. They drink their tea.

ANNA. Oh yes it's delicious…

Erm…

So, I don't know quite what Daphne told you…

Beat.

CORIN. Well, she told me a little.

ANNA. Well, it feels very odd to be having this conversation
with you but anyway.

She looks down into her tea for a second.

Well, Daphne said to me you'd been saying that it was
something you had been thinking about. That you'd never
wanted to before but now you've got to a certain stage and
suddenly it was something that interested you.

CORIN. Yes.

ANNA. Well, you're the first person I've spoken to, and,
obviously what I want, what would be exciting, is to do it
with someone interesting, someone talented. Obviously
you're both of those things.

Erm, I know you're also famous and that makes it difficult.

And I wanted to make it clear it's not about financial support,
if it made you feel more comfortable I could absolutely sign
something saying I wouldn't try to get money out of you, or

whatever, that it would all be confidential, or whatever you wanted.

The point is for me, what excites me is the idea of making a baby with someone interesting and talented.

CORIN. Yes.

Silence.

ANNA *tries not to fidget.* CORIN *sips, puts down his tea.*

How does it, how did you think it might happen?

ANNA. Um – do you mean – the –
The?

Beat.

Well, I've already gone a certain way, found a clinic, you can go to this clinic.
Registered as a couple which is much quicker, erm –
or, *you* can go to them and register as a sperm donor… so, um, you can do it in many ways.

Beat.

Or –
I suppose –
We could always, um,

Could always do it the, the er natural way.

CORIN *flinches slightly,* ANNA *immediately regrets this comment.*

There are many ways, there are many ways. Skin a cat.

Pause.

CORIN. Yes.

Pause.

Well as Daphne told you – she's right,
I am interested.
I am interested in the idea.
I do feel for you, Anna, I feel for your situation.

ANNA. Oh brilliant.

CORIN. And it's odd because as I was saying to Daphne, I've actually just been reading Knausgaard and I got to a passage, I was reading it on the plane on the way here actually and it's the passage where he describes the birth of his child and I found it incredibly moving.

ANNA. Really...

CORIN. I was in tears.
But the thing is I've got to be really clear here.

ANNA. Okay.

CORIN. Firstly.
I know I don't want to be a father.

Beat.

ANNA. Oh...?

CORIN. Yes. People always say oh but you will you will, but I know quite clearly I don't, I really do know myself.

Beat.

ANNA. Right then I don't think I quite –

CORIN. So if I were to do this then the child could never know I was the father.

Pause.

ANNA. Ah.

CORIN. And that might be fraught with difficulty as we do know some of the same people, we could end up at some garden party and there you are with a toddler and there I am – you see what I mean?

ANNA. ... Yes.

CORIN. And I know your parents, that's a whole other thing.

ANNA. Well, I'm sure they'd be thrilled, but.

CORIN. But.

ANNA. Hmmm.

Beat.

I don't know quite what to say…

Pause.

CORIN. It's important I make it clear I suppose.

ANNA. I see, thank you very much.

CORIN. I just know I don't want to be a father.

ANNA. Right. Thank you.

CORIN. But I do feel for your situation.

ANNA. Right.

CORIN. I am interested.

ANNA. Right.

CORIN. But I don't want to be a father.

ANNA. Okay.

Beat.

Maybe I should just think about what you've said.

CORIN. Yes. Do that.

Scene Eleven

39 + 5

The little GIRL *lies in the bed.* ANNA *sits on the edge of the bed.* ANNA*'s tone is as if she is reading aloud a story. In a different part of the stage,* LACHLAN *stands, smoking a cigarette.*

ANNA....So *then* what happened was, the Irish man whose sister had died, we met up and we went to the *ballet*.

GIRL. Why?

ANNA. So we didn't have to make eye contact. It was a *modern* ballet...

GIRL. I saw a lobster once with purple bands on its paws.

ANNA. Yeah... on its claws ... and then the Irish man... well all night long we were watching this ballet, we couldn't talk and when we got outside he turned to me and said –

LACHLAN. So listen, Anna, I'm really glad we met up again, cos I know a lot of time has passed since we last met and I haven't been in touch. But I'm feeling a lot better now.

Beat.

I hope there's no awkwardness between us.

ANNA *looks at him, trying to fathom what this means.*

ANNA. No, no, um... Of course not.

LACHLAN. It was lovely to see you again.

He turns, about to go. The little GIRL *speaks directly to* LACHLAN.

GIRL. But you haven't said yes or no!!

LACHLAN *looks at her, leaves.*

ANNA. Maybe it's easier for him that way.

His sister had just died.

GIRL. But then what happened?

ANNA. Well then there was the man who was a vegetarian…
but he just tried to kiss me.

GIRL. Rude.

ANNA. That's what he's like.

GIRL. And then what happened.

ANNA. Well then there was the famous film director… but he
never called me again.

GIRL. Why?

ANNA. I think I put him off when I said we could do it the
natural way.

GIRL.…I want another story.

Scene Twelve

39 + 6

ANNA *sits in a nice restaurant with* JULIE. JULIE *is about
ten or so years older than* ANNA *and speaks in an Australian
accent.*

JULIE.…But if Filippo had his way *neither* of us would
work… we would just stay at home together all day
watching shit telly.

ANNA. If only!

JULIE. Yes…

I think the trouble is the house has been really crowded with
the *boys* being back from uni and Filippo, I think that's been
doing his head in. Filippo, you know, he likes to have his
space, stay up very late, watching stuff, smoking and
thinking and stuff…

ANNA. Mmm.

JULIE. And my boys disrupt that... But luckily, they're going away with their dad and then we'll have the house to ourselves again. Filippo needs that.

ANNA. Yeah...

JULIE (*warmly*)....But Anna. How are *you* doing?

ANNA. Well...

You know... The break-up with Tom was really hard...

JULIE *sighs*.

JULIE. I know, Anna. I know. I'm so, so sorry about that.

JULIE*'s eyes fill with tears. She brushes one away.*

ANNA. Gosh... Julie... I...

JULIE. No, I'm so glad you got in touch. I've been thinking about you a lot... because of course, I've *seen* Tom...

Beat.

ANNA. How is he?

JULIE. Well... we saw him at a party... and it was funny, he looked... *younger*...

ANNA. I know.
It's like he's aged backwards since we broke up.

JULIE. But actually, I hardly talked to him. It was Filippo who talked to him. They went and smoked together.

ANNA. Yes, I heard Tom's started smoking again... how did Filippo say he was?

JULIE. He said Tom was trying to write something.

ANNA. Mmm. Yes.

JULIE. Anna. I felt so sad when I heard about you and Tom. I saw how happy you made him. You were so well-matched.

It's a terrible pity.

JULIE *is tearful again.*

ANNA. Yes... You know we were trying for a baby...

JULIE. I did know that, Anna, yes.

She squeezes ANNA*'s hand.*

I'm so sorry, Anna.

Pause.

ANNA. Yeah. It's difficult to know what to do now. I've been a bit of a mess, really.

JULIE. Yes. I know, I know.

ANNA. Asking people... if they can help me out... I don't really have time to fall in love with someone else...

JULIE. But you're so lovely, why do you think you won't meet someone... you will.

Beat.

ANNA. Well – I'm thirty-nine.

Beat.

JULIE. There is no right way of doing it, Anna. In a way I'm lucky I had mine so young... but then of course, the marriage didn't last.

The little GIRL *comes in, watches them from a slight distance.*

And of course, I sometimes worry that Filippo, you know, coming from an Italian family... and being younger than me, will want some of his own one day. Italians, it's all about the kids, the bambini. And of course, I can't any more. It's difficult every which way.

ANNA. Yes...

Pause.

Well actually, Julie –

Erm it's really difficult to know how to say this, but... Tom *did* mention, ages ago, I mean when we were going out with each other, that you were worried one day Filippo would want a kid of his own and...

God, this is very difficult...

JULIE....

ANNA. And I was thinking, and it occurred to me.

Well really, Julie, I wanted to run this by *you* first, but if Filippo *did* want to have a kid, he could give his... sperm... to, um to me.

Silence.

JULIE. Oh Anna... I don't know...

ANNA. No, I mean, forget it, forget it...

JULIE. No, it's just, Anna... having children with someone, it's an incredibly... it's the most intimate thing you can do.

Beat.

ANNA. Of course, of course...

JULIE. I'm just not sure we would... *survive* it, you know what I'm saying?

ANNA. Julie, of course. Of course. Please.

Beat.

I wish I hadn't asked.
I'm sorry. I feel I've ruined our lovely lunch now...

JULIE. No, no. Not at all.

Beat.

ANNA. Julie, I'm sorry to have asked... but I've been a bit desperate... I've asked lots of people, and... had no luck so far...

Beat.

I suppose I felt, I wouldn't ever know if I didn't ask, so, there was nothing to lose by asking.

Beat.

JULIE. But maybe you should have sat and thought a little harder before asking.

Beat.

ANNA. Um…

JULIE. I'm kind of surprised, Anna, that you didn't have more imagination about how I might feel.

Given your own situation.

GIRL. But you have two children.

ANNA. Oh I'm sorry, Julie…

JULIE. It's all very well that 'If you don't ask you don't get' approach but this isn't *crowdfunding* – don't you think it's dangerous when it's people's private lives you're asking about?
Lives you might know nothing about?

ANNA. I'm sorry.

GIRL. I don't want your husband…

Beat.

JULIE. You think I didn't *want* to have a child with Filippo?

GIRL. I don't have any.

Beat.

JULIE. Yes, if you don't ask 'You'll never know.' But you run the risk of causing other people pain. Opening up stuff they've tried to work through, get over, finally put away and managed to lay to rest.
Or not.

ANNA. Julie, I'm sorry.

JULIE. You don't really know me very well. In future maybe you should just try asking people you know a bit better.

She gets up and leaves.

GIRL (*after her*). I don't have anyone.

Interval.

Scene Thirteen

39 + 7

ANNA *sits in the kitchen with her friend* BETH, *drinking wine*.

BETH....I don't know, Anna... How many have you asked now?

ANNA *silently counts up on her fingers, saying names under her breath.*

ANNA....Oh no hang on...
... ...
...Eleven. They all said no.
It's weird, you sort of end up being a different version of 'you' with each one... The actors are up for it, I think because they're used to being asked to play *roles*... they *think* about it for a bit... 'Do I want this part' – then they say no.

PAUL *comes in, waving a mobile which is ringing. The ringtone is a duck quacking.* PAUL *is very softly spoken.*

PAUL. Sweetie – it's your mother.

BETH. I don't want to talk to her.

PAUL *puts down the phone, still quacking, leaves.*

...She's driving me crazy...

ANNA. Your mum is lovely...

BETH. My mum is mad, Anna. Sometimes I feel I don't know who she *is*. She's a full-blown hoarder now. You know she has *boxes* in her room. Piled up by the bed. With labels on.

She makes the inverted commas in the air.

'HOUSE.' 'DIVORCE.' 'NAZIS.'

ANNA....She's just trying to make sense of her life.

BETH. Why do I have to be *her* mother? She's *my* mother.

ANNA. She loves you. Every time you write an article, she sends it to everyone you know.

BETH. *Including* the editor who commissioned it!

ANNA (*thoughtfully*). Probably quite a good idea, actually.

The little GIRL *comes in with a storybook.*

GIRL. Will you come up, Mama?

BETH. No, darling. I've *been* up.

Leave me and Anna alone. This is grown-up time.

GIRL. Story?

BETH. No. You've had one.

GIRL. Please?

BETH. No means no.

ANNA (*to herself*). But *does* it…

BETH (*looking at the book*). Ugh, certainly *not* 'The Cave of Time'.

(*To* ANNA.) She's into these bloody 'choose your own adventure' books now. You know, alternative worlds. If you go through the red door, turn to page twenty-eight. I just don't want her to start asking me about free will versus predestination. (*To the* GIRL.) Off you go.
And check baby on your way up.

The GIRL *starts to go off. Shouts from off.*

GIRL (*from off*). *Keep the noise up!*

BETH (*throwing her voice*). Will do!

GIRL (*from off, further away*). *Love you!*

BETH (*throwing her voice*). Love you!

GIRL (*far away*). *All of it!*

BETH (*throwing her voice*). All of it!

GIRL (*faintly*). *And the rest!*

BETH (*throwing her voice*). And the rest!

…needs this ritual every night…

ANNA. I know… Sometimes *I* feel like I'm ten years old…

GIRL (*faintly*). *Mama!*

BETH. Yes!

GIRL (*faintly*). *Just checking!*

BETH. I don't know, Anna... What about the fucking *gays*? (*Throwing voice.*) *Love you!*

ANNA. Like who?

BETH. Well, I keep thinking *Zachary*... he'd be the perfect gay... intelligent, funny, successful career in New York...

ANNA. Yes, the same thought had crossed my mind...

BETH. The only thing is, he's your brother...

ANNA. Yes...

GIRL (*faintly*). *Mama!*

BETH. Yes!

GIRL (*faintly*). *Just checking!*

BETH. What about *Felix*? He's gay. Art dealer.

ANNA. a: I don't think Felix likes me very much, and b: I don't think he wants a child, so those are two quite big stumbling blocks. But actually, there is *one* gay friend, of Rosemary's –

BETH. Oh yes?

ANNA. 'Rupert', apparently he's *desperate* for a kid... bit older... writes graphic novels... incredibly keen... tried to twice, but the women let him down...

BETH. Oooooh... Dunno if I like the sound of that.

ANNA. What, graphic novels?

BETH. No, 'Incredibly keen'... He'll be wanting to get all involved. He'll want to deliver the baby.

ANNA. Isn't that the *point*?... Thing is, I tried reading one of his books...
and it wasn't very *good*... What if the kid asked me what I thought of Daddy's *writing*, what would I say? 'It's shit'?

BETH. Anna, for fuck's sake, that is the most *middle-class* fear
I've ever heard! You *have* to get away from your
upbringing...
But, I *do* wonder if you're not better off with a sperm
donor... you don't have to *agree* on everything, for a start...

PAUL *comes in.*

PAUL (*quietly*). I'm just ordering the pedal bin. Do we want
thirty-five litres or forty-five litres?

BETH. God, I don't know.

PAUL. Forty-five litres?

BETH. Just *buy* it. I want to talk to Anna.

PAUL. How are you, Anna?

BETH. I'm just telling her she should go with an anonymous
sperm donor so she doesn't have to *agree* on everything.

PAUL....Oh... I *know* someone who was the child of an
anonymous sperm donor. James. You should meet him.

ANNA. Is he gay?

PAUL. No. Have you heard anything from Tom?

BETH. Tom's history! Tom let her down! Tom's an arsehole!

PAUL. I just wondered how –

BETH. How *he* is? When he got together with Anna, he broke
up with his *mum*. And now they've just got back together
again!

PAUL. I feel sorry for him.

BETH. For *him*? *Why?*

PAUL. Well... Poor guy... I can kind of *see* why he freaked
out... He's allowed to feel the way he felt... Maybe he
was... just too young.

ANNA. Yeah... Look, for the record, *I* was freaked out too,
okay?... It's just, the thought of *not* having a kid made me
feel *more* freaked out, so... (*To* PAUL.) Do you think I've
gone mad? Asking all these men?

PAUL. I don't know. Have you gone mad?

BETH. Of course she's not gone *mad*! She's doing the only sane, logical thing she can do in an impossible situation!

PAUL. But that's the thing about madness, it poses itself as sanity.

BETH. Tom left her high and dry. So what, she's not going to have children – because of fucking *Tom*?

PAUL. But are you sure you want a child?

ANNA. Yes.

BETH. Of course she is!

PAUL. But *why* do you want a child?

Beat.

ANNA. I can't explain it.
Life just feels pointless without...

PAUL. What does that mean.

ANNA. I don't know. Without it feels like death.

PAUL. But what does that *mean*.

ANNA. I can't explain it.

Beat.

The awful thing is when people say you don't have a god-given right to a child – they're right...
I know there are people who are perfectly happy without.
I'm just not one of them.

BETH. Look, Anna. When you get your baby – and you will – you'll be so in love with it, you *just* have to think if you hadn't broken up with Tom you would never have had that particular wonderful baby. Everything happens for a reason.

ANNA. Yeah.
I used to think that.

Beat.

Actually, I have heard from Tom – he sent me this novel he's written.

BETH. Hopeless!

ANNA (*suddenly angry*). I know! I need sperm! Not a novel.
He inscribed it 'You were always my audience for all things
comic.' I mean, what!! 'You *were*...' Putting me in the past
tense! I'm not fucking *dead*! Novel wasn't even about me...
Sorry, I'm obviously still quite angry... I should really be past
that stage of grief by now... what *are* the stages of grief?

PAUL. Denial, anger, bargaining, depression and acceptance.

BETH (*suspiciously*). Wow.

PAUL. I've been reading this book. Apparently there are only
seven stories, every story is a variant on one of them. Rags to
Riches, Overcoming the Monster, Voyage and Return, The
Quest, / Tragedy –

BETH. / All right, all right!!... Don't *shout* at us!

He has not raised his voice.

I've been reading this book – *Are Men Obsolete* by Camille
Paglia.

The little GIRL *comes back in.*

PAUL. Well, I think that's all we need to know.

BETH. Oh sweetheart, *what*?

GIRL....My knee?

BETH *looks at her knee.*

BETH. Wonderful. Your scab is gone.

ANNA. I wish *my* scabs healed that quickly.

PAUL *takes the* GIRL*'s hand.*

PAUL. Come on. I'll tuck you in.

GIRL (*lingering*). I want *Anna* to tell me a story.

BETH. Anna has to finish telling *me* a story.

GIRL. I like *Anna's* stories.

BETH. So do I. She'll come up in five minutes. Anna?

ANNA. Sure.

As they are leaving.

PAUL. Night night!

GIRL. Night night!

BETH *and* ANNA. Night night! Sleep tight!
Night night!

PAUL *and the little* GIRL *leave. A brief pause.*

ANNA. You're so lucky to have children.

BETH. I don't 'have' children.

ANNA. Yes you do.

BETH. I don't, Anna.

ANNA. What do you mean?

BETH. I don't 'have' them. I don't *own* them. They are their
own people.

ANNA. You can only say that because you have them.

Scene Fourteen

39 + 8

ANNA *sits side by side with* RUPERT *and* PETE *in a
counsellor's office.* RUPERT *has an accent which is half-
London, half-posh. He is enthusiastic.* JENNY, *the counsellor,
a middle-aged woman, listens patiently.*

RUPERT.... The thing is my own upbringing was quite chaotic,
but I feel really confident that I *myself* can be a great dad.
I've also had a lot of contact with children through the books
I've written...

JENNY. So you're both creative!

ANNA. Yes...!

JENNY. Oh super... So, Rupert, have you talked with Anna
about how you would divide time with the child?

RUPERT. Oh yes! We've discussed it a lot. Me and Pete, our flat's quite near Anna's so that makes things easier already –

ANNA *is nodding*.

ANNA. Obviously it's hard when everything is still so hypothetical –

RUPERT. – but Pete and me *imagined* that the child would be living with Anna until at least two years old…

JENNY (*nodding*). And have you met Anna's family yet? Anna's brother Joe, he lives with her?

RUPERT. Oh yes I've met Anna's whole family…

JENNY. Really!

ANNA.… Yes…

RUPERT. In Bristol…

ANNA. My other brother Zachary was visiting from New York, he'd just broken up with his boyfriend so it felt like a good opportunity.

JENNY. And how did you feel around Anna's family, Rupert?

RUPERT. Extremely comfortable, very warm and welcoming. Quite original and quite eccentric, but I liked that, myself. Quite Chekhovian in a way… And Anna's mum said this amazing thing to me, she took me aside and she said how pleased they were that I was doing this, that I was doing this wonderful thing…

ANNA (*smiling*). Yes…

JENNY. So, Pete, as Rupert's partner, how do you feel about all this?

PETE. Yeah.

RUPERT. Pete knows I've wanted kids forever. Pete's younger than myself but he gets it.

PETE. Yeah.

RUPERT. Okay, it took him a little while to get his *head* around it, this has all happened relatively fast, but he's *totally* on-board now –

PETE. Yeah I am.

RUPERT. – strangely enough I'd actually sort of broken down a few months ago –

PETE. Yeah –

RUPERT. – told him that having a child was something I couldn't give up on, and he said okay –

PETE. I did.

JENNY. Rupert, you mentioned on the form that you have suffered from OCD.

Beat.

RUPERT. Very mild, very very mild. In the past, yes, but very mild. I was anxious basically. Under a lot of stress. Years ago.

Pause. JENNY *looks at her notes, nodding. Looks up.*

JENNY. …How do you feel about being an older dad? Are you at all *anxious* about that?

RUPERT. Erm… I suppose it's only natural yes because it's so unknown, but I think the anxiousness is a *version* of excitement. So… I'd say I'm *excited* really. That's how I'd put it. Excited about being an older dad.

PETE. Yeah.

RUPERT. I mean yes, I suppose I have days, nights actually, moments in the night when I've worried about the fact that I'll be an older dad. But I'm okay with it.

PETE. Yeah.

RUPERT. …Obviously it's a weird situation. But every time I've felt anxious, Anna and I have talked and I've felt better.

ANNA. The thing about Rupert is he is a genuinely kind person and for me that's the most important thing.

RUPERT. You're kind too, Anna.

ANNA. Thank you…

Pause. JENNY *looks at her notes again.*

JENNY. Anna, before when I saw you, you were considering using a sperm donor.

ANNA. Yes.

JENNY. And you didn't seem quite ready to do that, I thought.

ANNA. Yes...

JENNY. You had a lot of questions.

ANNA. Yes...

JENNY. You were still grieving your previous relationship, I thought.

ANNA.... That's probably true.

JENNY. How are you feeling now?

ANNA. Very different. The great thing about Rupert is that the child will know who their father is from the start. So I feel very good about it.

RUPERT. We feel very confident.

She smiles.

JENNY. Good luck.

Scene Fifteen

39 + 9

ANNA *and* RUPERT *are outside somewhere, holding small tubs of ice cream.*

RUPERT *is distressed.*

RUPERT. Honestly this is the first time I've been able to talk about it without crying, it's been that bad...

His eyes fill with tears.

Oh God...

It's just become untenable, I mean... the *anxiety...* untenable...

...I'm just filled with this *terror...*

ANNA *puts down her ice cream, wearily.*

ANNA. Right... I mean if it helps, Rupert, I feel scared too –

RUPERT (*obliviously*). Feeling I had to *prove* myself, with the counsellor, meeting your family... and I think it was that moment, that moment when your *mother* said that *thing* to me, about what a wonderful thing I was doing, at that moment I felt this immense *terror...* and I sort of knew *then...*

ANNA. Oh...

RUPERT. ...And then *Pete* said this thing ... if you're *this* worried are you sure you should be doing it and then I had a *huge* row with *Pete* and accused him of being unsupportive...

ANNA. Ah...

RUPERT. And I just realised I had to stop this. I had to stop. Before I lost it completely.

PETE comes on holding a little rucksack.

PETE. There wasn't any water. Shall I... go again?

RUPERT. Yes, yes.

PETE. You're okay?

RUPERT. Yes. I'm fine. It's fine. Go and look at the sculptures.

PETE (*kindly*). Anna. Are you okay?

ANNA. I'm fine, Pete, don't worry.

PETE *gives her a hug*.

RUPERT. Pete, we're fine.

PETE. I'll go and look at the sculptures.

He goes.

RUPERT. So I went to see that counsellor again –

ANNA. *Seriously?!* I hated that fucking counsellor –

RUPERT. Well, that's the thing, *you* always hated her, I thought she was nice.

And *she* said to me if I'm feeling like this I *absolutely* shouldn't go through with it.

Beat.

ANNA. Okay.

Beat.

Well, if that's the way you feel.

Pause.

RUPERT. I feel so bad.

Beat.

(*Gently.*) Rosemary told me a bit about, how you've been let down before…

ANNA *shifts uneasily.*

And I feel this terrible sadness myself at not doing it… but I can't. The thing is – I feel so bad for you. I really, really like you. But I can't do something just because I feel bad for you. This is my life.

ANNA. Okay.

Beat.

I'm sorry, Rupert, I, I hear all of this and you'll have to forgive me, I don't have the energy left for much reaction.

RUPERT. I feel so bad... I met your family and everything... Prosecco...

ANNA *tries to pull herself together*

ANNA (*dully*). Well... don't worry. They won't hate you. They're not like that. In fact my dad would probably understand how you felt, he felt very ambivalent when my mum got pregnant with –

RUPERT *explodes, shouting at her.*

RUPERT. But *Anna*, your father is *married* to your mother! He's *married* to her!

Our situation is totally different, Anna!!

ANNA (*shocked*). For fuck's sake, Rupert...!

Beat.

Jesus Christ, I'm trying to make an effort here, *I'm* actually trying to make *you* feel *better* –

Her voice starts to shake.

I don't think you realise how hard – I'm having to try – not to – not to –

She can't speak. RUPERT*'s tone changes abruptly to pity.*

RUPERT....Oh God, just look at us... we're just two people, just standing here who can't really help one another, two people just causing one another pain...

ANNA (*erupting*). What the *fuck*?? What pain have I caused you? *All* I have done is listen to you talk for forty minutes and tried to be as understanding as I can! I've had enough of this. You have wasted my time. I don't want to waste a minute longer.
I have to go.
I have to make phone calls.
I have to make lists.
I have to find someone who will help me.

She leaves.

Scene Sixteen

39 + 10

ANNA *sits with her* MOTHER *at a laptop.*

ANNA. Okay, Mum.
I've reached a point where… I think I have to do this.
And I want you to help me choose.

MOTHER. Okay.

Pause.

I think that it's *good*, Pippy.

ANNA. Do you?

MOTHER. Yes, it is. I think the sperm-donor thing is amazing.
We never had that option. When I think how close I came to
never having you…

ANNA. Yeah…

MOTHER. Dad was adamant he didn't want children. What if
the coil had done its job? What if you hadn't happened?

ANNA.… Well, I did.

MOTHER. But if I hadn't had *you*, he would never have seen
the point, and then we wouldn't have gone on to have Zach,
Joe…

DAD *comes in eating a lump of cheese.*

DAD. Somebody stop me eating this cheese…

ANNA. I thought you were fasting today.

DAD. I am.

MOTHER.… I could have ended up childless. The point is, *you*
don't, actually, have to do it with a man, Anna, you don't
have to make a man *agree* to have children, thank God.

DAD. Men don't have to agree for it to happen! (*To* ANNA.)
You're the living proof! I'm eating this cheese. I didn't agree
for it to happen.

MOTHER. I think this sperm-donor thing is a wonderful
development. O brave new world.

ANNA. Yeah well. If you look below the line on the *Telegraph* website. 'Selfish women' blah blah blah. 'Pleasing *themselves*' blahblahblah. I mean do they think that *men* have nothing to do with having to do it this way?

DAD. It is a perfectly reasonable position not to want children! Look, I'm all in favour of it – *now* – but that doesn't change the fact that it doesn't make sense to *do* it. I mean think of the act of childbirth, for God's sake... (*To* MOTHER.) Remember when you gave birth to Anna?

MOTHER (*lighting up*). Oh *yes*... I didn't know what I was doing at all, but there was this wonderful midwife –

DAD. What are you talking about? She wasn't wonderful, she was awful!

MOTHER (*genuinely flummoxed*). Really? The way I remember it, we arrived, and it was all going rather slowly, and then the midwife did a sweep to get things moving –

DAD. Because she was an old-school torturer! Women don't stand a chance, you're cannon-fodder. Why the hell did she give you an episiotomy?

MOTHER (*uncertainly*). Well, I don't remember, exactly –

DAD. Because you were zonked out on Pethedine, you remember nothing! She did it because they like doing it, it seems to me, they've been doing it since the thirteenth century –

ANNA. Why do you keep interrupting her?!

DAD. Because she can't remember what it was like!
(*To* MOTHER.) I remember *everything*, they had to work the scissors round your head, Anna, the midwife's knuckles went white –

MOTHER. Really...? I just remember her talking about her holidays...

DAD. Yeah, I had to tell her to shut up, like a fucking *cabbie*, if you're giving birth you have to concentrate!

ANNA. Of course, you'd know all about it.

DAD. I *do*.

MOTHER. All *I* remember, Anna, is that you finally came out, and I was so happy… but then I worried because your eyes were shut for so long…

ANNA. How long?

MOTHER. About a week. A miracle, there you were, conceived in spite of the coil…

DAD. You came out holding it in your hand…

MOTHER. *Your* generation, well, it's fucking difficult for you lot. Blokes can get sex without marriage… sex without children…

DAD. Not true. No one is more henpecked than a man being given a blowjob.

ANNA. Yeah, and even when they're *gay*, they freak out like they're straight… bloody *Rupert*…

MOTHER. Oh, *Rupert*…

ANNA. Well. At least it meant I didn't have to read his graphic novels.

DAD (*to* MOTHER). You know what Zach said about that lunch when Rupert came to meet us? He said he was looking at him thinking – (*Triumphantly.*) 'At last. It's *Anna*, not me, who has to bring home her gay boyfriend.' (*Laughs.*) And every time Rupert said something gay, he'd wince inside and think, 'Ooch! *That* was a bit camp!' And then he'd think, 'Not my problem!'

MOTHER. That reminds me, I'd better transfer Zach some money…

ANNA. Muum… he earns more than the rest of us put together… your relationship with Zach is very codependent, do you realise?

MOTHER. 'Codependent?' You mean I need to give him *more* money?

ANNA *and* DAD. No!!

DAD. – Jesus!

ANNA. Codependent means… he depends on you giving him money and you depend on him to… feel motherly.

MOTHER *(happily)*. Oh, we're *definitely* codependent in that case.

DAD. It's not a *good* thing.

ANNA *is tapping on her laptop.*

ANNA. So I've narrowed it down to two donors…

DAD. What, you're *still* on this?? I already told you which one, months ago!!

ANNA. I know, but I want to see which one Mum chooses.

DAD. Why? She's got terrible judgement. What's wrong with the one I chose? I liked him. I *invested* in him. He had a grin just like Joe.

ANNA. Well, obviously a popular choice.

MOTHER. His spunk sold out while she was dicking around with Rupert.

ANNA *has pulled up a page.*

ANNA. Okay. Here's the first. Some Italian –

DAD. Mozzarella.

ANNA. – and some Mexican blood.

DAD. Tacos.

ANNA. Quite handsome. Not a bad intelligence score.

Beat.

MOTHER. Okay.
Now show me the other.

ANNA *taps.*

ANNA. Sweet face, medium intelligence, some Cajun blood.

DAD. Mmm. I'm salivating.

Beat.

MOTHER (*decisively*). No.
　　I like the other one better.
　　I don't like this one's face.

　　Beat.

ANNA (*admiringly*).... Wow, Mum! I had no idea you could be
　　so *ruthless*!

DAD. Fuck are you talking about? The woman is lethal.

ANNA. No, seriously!
　　If only you'd been like that about some of my *boyfriends*...
　　Okay... there we go then... 349087, it's your lucky day...
　　(*Tapping at the laptop*.) I'll put in an order...

DAD (*about to leave, he turns back*). Which reminds me. We
　　need to do an Ocado. And something, I'm not sure if it's
　　raspberries, has leaked in the freezer, it looks like someone's
　　been whaling, it's all blood and ice in there. (*On his way out,
　　throwing his voice*.) We need ginger beer. The diet one. It's
　　just as nice.

　　He goes out. ANNA *taps at the laptop. Half to herself.*

ANNA. It's weird... when you think of all these children that
　　could have come into being with all those different men I
　　asked... but didn't... all those lives that were never started...

　　Pause.

MOTHER. Have you spoken to Tom at all?

ANNA. There's no point. He's made up his mind.

MOTHER. But the thing is, Pippy.

　　Beat.

　　Did you ever *really* let rip? Really let him know how you
　　feel, let him *know* what a terrible thing he's done to you?

ANNA. Erm...

　　Beat.

　　...Well, once, sort of, but actually I felt that letting rip was
　　only pushing him away and at that point I was trying to do
　　anything I could to... get him back. So I stopped.

MOTHER. But he *hasn't* changed his mind, so at this stage, what have you got to lose?

ANNA. Fucking hell... my equilibrium... my pride...

MOTHER. Oh, *pride*, Pippy really... amour-propre, what's the *point*, _really_?

ANNA. Dad thinks talking to him again is absolutely pointless.

MOTHER. But I think Tom has to know. What you feel. Why don't you try telling him?

Beat.

ANNA. When have you ever told Dad what you feel? About all the shit he's done?

Pause.

MOTHER.... Well. He doesn't want to hear.

ANNA. Well then.

Beat.

MOTHER. Pippy – what Tom's *done* – I don't think he doesn't love you. I think he is just scared. Scared of his fucking horrible mother who is a bitch.

ANNA.... I had a terrible dream where I said to his mum, 'You are a fucking cunt.'

MOTHER. What did she say?

ANNA. We were in a foyer. Someone was trying to introduce us and I said, 'I know who you are. You are a fucking cunt.'

MOTHER. Well, she is a fucking cunt.

ANNA (*sighing*). No, she's his *mum*. She was protecting him. You want to protect your kid. She just happened to be protecting him from me.

MOTHER. No, I honestly do think it's all her fault! She is a very powerful woman who dominates all her children and Tom would have been *fine* –

ANNA (*sharply*). So what are you saying about where I am now? If Tom and me would have been fine, if only it hadn't

been for his mum? What the hell does that say about where
I am *now*?

Beat.

MOTHER *(carefully)*. Okay. If you're asking me.

ANNA. Yes, I am asking you.

Beat.

MOTHER *(slowly)*. I think what has happened… is a tragedy.

ANNA *(flaring up)*. *Mum!!* I can't think of it as a *tragedy*! I can't
go around thinking, 'My life is a tragedy.' 'I'm *tragic*.' Don't
you understand? Fucking hell… I'm trying to be *positive*
here… I thought you said it was *good* I'm doing it with a
sperm donor…

She starts crying. MOTHER *is distressed.*

MOTHER. Oh, Pippy, I'm sorry… I just *do*, I *do* think it's a
tragedy, I feel terribly sorry for you, I just think life has been
extremely unfair and difficult for you… Oh, Pippy… come
and sit on my lap…

ANNA *rather unwillingly sits on her lap and her* MOTHER
rocks her backwards and forwards as she cries.

There, there… it'll be okay…

ANNA *(angrily)*. How can it be okay if it's a *tragedy*??

MOTHER. Shhh… shhhhhh…

After a bit ANNA *manages to speak.*

ANNA. Of course I miss him… I miss his tiny handwriting…
I found a recipe for *pizza* dough he'd written the other day…
But… maybe the way I have to think about it is… Beth said,
the child who, touch wood, I will have… obviously I'll love
it… I just have to think… *that* child would never have
existed if Tom and I hadn't broken up…?

MOTHER *(worried)*.…Oh no, Annie, I don't think that's
right… I don't think you can lay all that on a *child*… to
redeem your *life*… plus the child will come with its *own*
problems –

ANNA *springs up*.

ANNA. Fucking *hell*, Mum! You're so *negative*! I am trying to find some way forward in this mess! Don't you *give* a shit?

Now the MOTHER *is hurt*.

MOTHER (*her voice trembling*). Of *course* I give a shit! I care *desperately* about you and what has been happening to you!

Tears rise up.

I… At night I lie there and I… *pray*… for you… I *pray* that everything will turn out okay for you…

The MOTHER *cries for a minute*. ANNA *watches. She is ashamed*.

ANNA. Oh, Mum… I'm sorry… I'm sorry…

She hugs her.

Come on… sit on *my* lap…

The MOTHER *sits somewhat unsteadily on* ANNA*'s lap*.

It'll be okay. Shhh… Shh…

There, there…

Actually sit a bit further here cos you're hurting my knees… that's it…

Do you remember this…

She starts to sing, rocking in time.

'You are my sunshine, my only sunshine…'

MOTHER. Of *course* I care about you…

ANNA. I know you do… Shhh…

I'll buy this sperm and I'll do it and it will be okay.

There's just one more person I've got to meet before I do…

Beat.

MOTHER. When you have a child, Anna, you will get to see all the bits of your life you've forgotten about. The first time you tasted a lemon. You get to relive it all again.

ANNA. Yeah…
    I keep thinking about Natasha…

MOTHER. What about Natasha…

ANNA. When she was dying in hospital, she thought she was in a Nazi concentration camp.
    She wanted me to feed her apple puree.

    Beat.

MOTHER. And did you?

ANNA. Feed her apple puree? Yes.

MOTHER. Good.

ANNA. She didn't want to die.

Scene Seventeen

39 + 11

ANNA *sits in a café with* JAMES. *His manner has an odd formality.* ANNA *is looking at her watch.*

ANNA. You absolutely mustn't be late… how the hell did you get tickets?

JAMES. I have a friend who helped with the video projection.

ANNA. He *is* quite good.

JAMES. Well, it is the role, isn't it… that every actor wants to play…

ANNA.… Yeah, I'm just not quite sure whether he has the *darkness* for Hamlet but…

    Anyway I'll shut up.

    Beat.

    Well, I have to tell you I've already bought the donor sperm.

    Beat.

But when you emailed back I thought I should meet you anyway because at the start of this whole thing I looked online and what stopped me then was there seem to be a lot of disturbed kids out there who are donor conceived so...

Beat.

I just wondered, well really – um...

Beat.

I know it's a stupidly big question, but, how have *you* found it?

Pause.

JAMES. Which parent did you want to be like?

Beat.

ANNA. Erm... I actually worried about turning into *either* of them... I wanted to be like my – well, I didn't want to be like my dad exactly, because my mother is a lovely person...

Beat.

But I wanted to achieve like my dad...
Sorry, it sounds a bit confused, doesn't it...

Beat.

I get on with them both, I get on with them both.

Beat.

When did you... find out?

JAMES. Um, my mum told me when I was four, I think.

Beat.

She told me a story, a sort of extended metaphor about a farmer and seeds in a field.
...I was happy. I was okay with it. She... conveyed to me the lengths to which she had gone to get me, and I felt wanted. I felt happy.

ANNA. Oh good.

JAMES. Yeah... It only started to prey on my mind when I was about thirteen...

ANNA. Oh right...

JAMES. Then more and more until I was eighteen and it was becoming a sort of obsession...

ANNA. Oh...

JAMES. So in the end I went to the clinic where she'd done it, and I tracked down this file. And there was a tick when she'd got pregnant. And this number. And they said that's the sperm donor.

He takes a sip of tea, ANNA *waits.*

ANNA. Did it... did you feel better?

Beat.

JAMES. If anything I felt worse after that. It sort of made it worse.

ANNA. Oh dear...

Pause.

JAMES. I registered with the donor network in case he were ever to contact them to make his identity known.
I mean it's not going to happen, but.

ANNA. Well...

JAMES. I tried talking to a therapist...

Beat.

It's all about identity really. My identity felt very female. I didn't know how to be a man. I'd look at men to see how they hold their glass and drink their beer...

Beat.

I've been out with a lot of crazy broken girls. Probably trying to rewrite the relationship with my mum. Trying to mend it.

ANNA. Was she crazy and broken?

JAMES. In some ways...

ANNA. But... Paul said you have a kid?

JAMES. Yes. Me and my partner, we've got two now. First my son – and now my daughter is two.

ANNA. Did, did that not help at all? I mean, help you, the way you feel?

Beat.

JAMES. I suppose, in a way.
In that… I've tried to be the dad I've always wanted.

Beat.

I was teaching him how to make scrambled eggs today. We're growing courgettes together. I went kayaking with him over the summer. I'm kind of trying to do it how I read in books.

ANNA. Wow, that sounds much better than *my* dad.
I only remember my dad playing rugby in the park with us. And that was because it was only once.

Beat.

What was it like when your son was born… you must have been very nervous?

Beat.

JAMES. Yeah…

It's not Disney you know… you're expecting a Disney-esque thing… but he was this huge angry-looking… covered with blood… *huge* testicles like very mature figs… he was very big, they lifted him up out of her like a – (*Gestures.*) great fish… this messy angry looking creature, purple, really dark purple, dense dark curly hair, matted with blood, it's been wet for nine months, it goes densely curly, he looked African in origin, he didn't look Caucasian. I actually thought am I the dad?

… And this thing emerges from her body and then it's feeding from her body… but then… your role as a man comes into the picture a bit later on.

Beat.

The thing is with your kid you can be silly, with kids any situation can be made to be funny. The other day, I had dinner in a restaurant with my daughter even though she's two. And it was sort of romantic… you can be silly and *romantic* with your kids.

ANNA. That's lovely.

Beat.

What was your stepfather like?

Pause.

JAMES. Well, he's dead now.

ANNA. Oh.

JAMES. Yes I basically had to look after him. He was ill and dying and he was sleeping on the sofa. He'd cry out in the night and say, 'I'm scared to die' and I would hold him. And I wondered why he couldn't do that for me.

He is suddenly close to tears.

ANNA. What, did he not...

JAMES. He never held me while I was growing up.

Beat.

A child – needs – to be held by their father.

He tears up again.

I look for my father on the Underground. My eyes go from man to man thinking 'Are you my father?' 'Are you my father?' 'Are you my father?'

They say donor. I say my father.
I have to claim that. I have to claim that word.

ANNA. Yes...

Beat.

So do you really think...

JAMES. I think it's very harmful to the child.

ANNA (*quietly*). Shit...

Silence.

JAMES. What do you think you're going to do?

Scene Eighteen

40

ANNA *sits in a pub with* FELIX. *She has opened a bag of crisps and they both absent-mindedly eat from it.* FELIX *has a big square flat parcel wrapped in brown paper.*

ANNA. Thank you for coming all the way to me.

FELIX. Not at all. Not *at* all. I just came straight from picking this up. (*The parcel.*) I think he's quite promising. Watercolourist. We'll see.

ANNA. Did you have a good time at Jamie's fortieth?

FELIX. Oh, yes. Although I shouldn't have gone back to their house afterwards. Felt shit the next day.

ANNA. Have some more crisps, I'm eating them all...

FELIX. Thanks...

ANNA. So listen, Felix... Sorry to be so mysterious...

FELIX. No, no...

ANNA. I'll be quick.
I've been trying to find a man to have a baby with. I asked lots of men and they all said no, then I thought I'd found a gay man, Rupert, and we went through all the counselling together, then he got scared and pulled out, not literally, well, practically. Then I bought donor sperm. Then I met the child of a sperm donor who urged me not to use donor sperm. So I thought... I should try... just one more time... and ask... Is it something... you would... be interested in? Doing?

Beat.

FELIX. Yes.

Beat.

ANNA (*taken aback*). What, yes you would be interested in doing it?

FELIX. Yes.

ANNA. Erm, yes, you'd like to think about it?

FELIX. No, I don't need to think about it. Yes, I'd like to do it.

Pause.

ANNA. Bloody hell.

Beat.

FELIX. I'm saying 'Yes.'

ANNA. Fucking hell… you're the first guy to say that.
You're the first guy not to say you need to think about it.

Beat.

Felix – I have to tell you, strange things happen to men when they say they'll do this. They stop sleeping… they get incredibly anxious… they fall into a depression… and then, they say they can't do it.

FELIX. I don't think I'll do that.

Beat.

ANNA. I think I should offer you a little more time to think about it.

FELIX. I don't need time to think about it.

ANNA. But I think you should. Just in case you develop insomnia or whatever.

FELIX. Okay. What about a week?

ANNA. Okay. Wow.

FELIX. I don't think I'll change my mind.

He smiles at her.

I mean –

It's the point of life, isn't it?

Scene Nineteen

26

Years earlier. ANNA, *wearing a coat, stands in a hospital ward. The 'silence' of hospital air – i.e. a faint hum, bleeping, sporadic shuffling footsteps. There are three beds. Two are empty. In the third lies* NATASHA, *an old woman. Her eyes are closed. She is obviously dying.* ANNA *approaches, tentatively, carrying a plastic bag of food. Her phone vibrates in her pocket. She picks up the call. Speaks quietly.*

ANNA. Hi… Hey…

No, I'm just… I'm visiting Natasha.

…I thought –

Yeah. She looks like she's not awake at the moment.

…Yeah, I brought her some stuff.

The phone wedged between shoulder and ear, she shifts the bag from one hand to another – it's heavy.

Okay.

Listen, Jugsy… Jugsy, wait – I've – I don't think I'm meant to be on my phone here, there are loads of signs.

Okay. I'll call you when I get back out.

Bye.

She ends the call. Goes the few remaining steps to NATASHA. *Sits gingerly on the plastic seat next to the bed. Looks at* NATASHA *a moment. Decides to take a few things out of her bag. One is a jar of shop-bought apple puree. She has also bought Actimel, rice pudding, etc.…*

NATASHA *stirs.*

Natasha…?

NATASHA *doesn't speak. After a bit her eyes slowly half-open.*

Hi…

Are you awake?

It's Anna…

Pause.

I came to bring you something nice to eat…

NATASHA *speaks in a dry whisper throughout the scene.*

NATASHA.… Yes…

ANNA. Are you alright?

Pause.

NATASHA.… Yes…

ANNA. Are you… comfortable like that?

Pause.

NATASHA.… Yes…

Beat.

ANNA. I brought you some more apple puree… you liked it, remember…

Do you want some?

Just the sound of NATASHA*'s breathing.*

ANNA *looks at her uncertainly.*

Okay…

Well…

I think you should have some… some water.

It's strawberry flavoured…

She gets a straw, puts it into a water bottle, gives it to NATASHA. *The straw hangs from* NATASHA*'s lips at a rakish angle. A pause.* NATASHA *seems to drink a tiny bit. The straw falls from her lips.*

Pause.

NATASHA (*quietly*). Nice…

Her eyes close.

ANNA. I told you so...

She takes the water bottle, watches NATASHA. *Pause. The little* GIRL *comes in.*

GIRL (*quietly*). Where am I...?

No one answers her. She sits down on the third bed, watches.

ANNA. How are you... feeling?

Pause. NATASHA *speaks quietly.*

NATASHA. I bought my house... in 1966.

ANNA (*hopefully*). Yes...!

...What was it like?

NATASHA. There was a sandpit in the garden.

Pause.

The couple before had two children.

ANNA. Lovely.

Pause. NATASHA*'s eyes open. The little* GIRL *perches on the bed, looks about.*

GIRL. I don't like it here...

NATASHA*'s eyes swivel to the far end of the room. Referring to someone –*

NATASHA (*weakly*). That one's trying to convert me to Catholicism...

ANNA (*firmly*). Nonsense.

NATASHA (*darkly, indicating the same person*). They shaved her head.

ANNA. ...No... She's... (*Lowers her voice.*) It's her chemotherapy...

Beat.

NATASHA. They're killing us.

ANNA. No no no. They're not.

She feels NATASHA*'s forehead.*

You feel a bit hot…

Pause. Both the little GIRL *and* NATASHA *heave a long sigh, in unison, the little* GIRL *lies back on her bed.*

NATASHA. If I am hot that means I am a Catholic.

Pause. NATASHA*'s eyes close again.*

ANNA. Do you want something to eat?

But NATASHA *seems to have exhausted herself from the exchange.*

GIRL.…I'm not hungry…

…Am I dying?

Pause. ANNA *puts aside the water bottle, uncertainly looks at the jar of apple puree. Opens it – looks at* NATASHA. *It seems an impossible task. Puts the lid on again.*

NATASHA (*faintly*).…Anna…

ANNA (*alertly*). Yes?

NATASHA.…I thought you'd gone.

ANNA. No no. I'm here. I'm still here.

A pause. Both NATASHA *and the little* GIRL *sigh again and move their right hand in unison.*

Maybe… just a spoonful?

But NATASHA *seems to be asleep again.*

GIRL.…I want to go home…

Pause.

ANNA (*quietly, to herself*). Why won't you *eat* anything…

NATASHA (*her eyes still shut, quietly*). I want to die…

ANNA (*hopelessly*). Please don't say that…

NATASHA. I want to die…

ANNA....But... don't you want to die at home?

Pause. With great weariness.

NATASHA. It's the end.

Silence. ANNA doesn't know what to say.

She strokes NATASHA's hand. Strokes her cheek.

ANNA. Poor Natasha... poor Natasha...

*With effort, NATASHA says something indistinguishable.
ANNA cranes in.*

What? What did you say?

Again, something indistinguishable.

...Do you want...?

Effortfully, NATASHA speaks –

NATASHA. Regrets...

ANNA.... 'Regrets'?

Beat.

GIRL *(slowly, sleepily)*....Children... There was a sandpit in
the garden. They had two children.

*Beat. This upsets ANNA. She struggles with herself
a minute, on the brink of tears.*

ANNA. Well...
Well... You've... you've got me.

She takes NATASHA's hand.

GIRL. It's the end of the story. No more story.

She pulls the blanket over herself. A long pause.

NATASHA....Anna?

ANNA. Yes.

NATASHA....I thought you'd gone.

ANNA. I'm still here.

Pause.

NATASHA.... Anna?

ANNA. Yes.

I'm still here.

Pause.

NATASHA (*sleepily*)....Just checking...

GIRL. Keep the noise up...

*The little GIRL sleeps. NATASHA's eyes stay closed.
ANNA waits. Lights fade.*

Scene Twenty

40

*Darkness. ANNA is lying in a pool of light, on a bed in her
outfit from the first scene. She has taken off her shoes but is
otherwise fully clothed. There is a vase of daffodils by the bed.
A watercolour propped nearby. She is reading a newspaper.
Silence but for the rustling of the newspaper.*

Then, noises from off.

*Suddenly FELIX comes in. He's holding a small transparent
plastic cup and is doubled up with laughter.*

FELIX. Here...!!

*He gives it to her. He can't stop laughing. ANNA smiles,
slightly bewildered.*

I'm *sorry*... it's so... such a small... tiny... *pathetic* amount!

But... my *mum* called... at the *crucial* moment... rather put
me off my stride...

'Mum'... flashing up on my phone... you know...

He dissolves into slightly hysterical laughter again.

ANNA (*laughing*). Oh my God...

FELIX. Yes... But... you know... it only takes one, correct?

ANNA. Absolutely.

A sudden pause.

Well... Felix... I'm going to strip off and lie with my legs in the air now, so...

FELIX. Absolutely, absolutely. I'll leave you to it.

He goes to leave. As he leaves.

And...
We'll just see what happens!

ANNA. Yes!

He is gone. ANNA is alone on the bed with the little cup in her hand. She looks at it. As the lights start to dim on her, very faintly, lights come up on the two beds from the previous scene, either side of her. One with NATASHA in it. One with the little GIRL asleep in it.

Lights hold on the three of them, each lying on their bed.

Fade to black.

The End.

www.nickhernbooks.co.uk

facebook.com/nickhernbooks

twitter.com/nickhernbooks